THE GOSPEL ACCORDING TO ST. MARK

NEW TESTAMENT FOR SPIRITUAL READING

Edited by

John L. McKenzie

THE GOSPEL
ACCORDING TO ST. MARK

Volume 2

/3572

RUDOLF SCHNACKENBURG

SHEED & WARD
LONDON AND SYDNEY

SHEED AND WARD LIMITED
33 Maiden Lane, London WC2E 7LA
and Sheed & Ward Pty. Limited,
204 Clarence Street, Sydney, N.S.W. 2000

Original edition: *Das Evangelium nach Markus, 2,* from
the series *Geistliche Schriftlesung,* edited by Wolfgang
Trilling in cooperation with Karl Hermann Schelkle and
Heinz Schürmann, Düsseldorf, Patmos-Verlag, 1970.
Translated by W. J. O'Hara.

Nihil Obstat: J. M. T. BARTON, DD, LSS, Censor
Imprimatur: ✠ VICTOR GUAZZELLI, Vic. Gen.
Westminster 6th July 1971

1970 by Patmos-Verlag
English translation © 1971 by Sheed and Ward, Limited.
SBN 7220 0419 2
Printed in the Republic of Ireland by Cahill & Co., Limited.

OUTLINE

Part 2: The Redemption (8:31—16:20)

THE ACCOMPLISHMENT OF REDEMPTION THROUGH JESUS' CROSS AND
RESURRECTION (8:31—16:8)

I. The initiation of the disciples into the mystery of the death
of the Son of man (8:31—10:45)

  1. The first prediction of the Passion and accompanying
  passages (8:31—9:29)

  2. The second prediction of the Passion and a collection of
  sayings for the Church (9:30–50)

  3. Important themes of concern to the Church, and the
  third prediction of the Passion (10:1–45)

II. Jesus' entry into Jerusalem and his last ministry in the
capital (10:46—13:37)

  1. Jesus' symbolic messianic ministry on arrival in Jerusalem
  (10:46—11:25)

  2. Controversy with leading circles in Jerusalem (11:27—
  12:44)

  3. The great apocalyptic discourse (chapter 13)

I

III. The Passion, death, and resurrection of Jesus (14:1—16:8)

1. The opponents' plot, the anointing in Bethany, the Last Supper, Gethsemane and arrest (14:1–52)

2. The proceedings against Jesus (14:53—15:15)

3. Way of the cross, death, and resurrection (15:16—16:8)

4. The longer ending of Mark (16:9–20)

PART 2

THE REDEMPTION
(8:31—16:20)

THE ACCOMPLISHMENT OF REDEMPTION THROUGH JESUS' CROSS AND RESURRECTION (8:31—16:8)

The net result of Jesus' public ministry was negative (8:27–30), but this outward failure was foreseen in God's saving plan. Jesus "must" take the way of the cross (8:31) in order "to give his life as a ransom for many" (10:45). Only in this way will the redemption of mankind be accomplished through the blood of this one man; through his blood God wills to establish a new covenant with the whole world (14:24). The reason for Jesus' frequently perplexing behavior earlier is now clear. His withdrawal from the crowd which applauded but did not understand his cures and mighty works, his demands for silence from those he cured and who proclaimed him a wonder worker, and from the devils who wanted to give away his secret for their own evil purposes, his reproof of the disciples for their lack of understanding—all this was done with knowledge of the death that was to befall him and which had been enjoined on him as necessary to transform the lot of sinful human beings, in whom there is still no change of heart. Jesus is now entering on his road to death, so he no longer needs to hide his "messianic secret." On the contrary, from this point onwards increasing light is thrown on the mystery that envelops his person. His hidden divine being is disclosed in anticipation to three trusted disciples (transfiguration, 9:2–13), blind Bartimeus is allowed to hail him openly as the Son of David (10:46–52), Jesus enters Jerusalem as the messianic bringer of peace (11:1–11), speaks of himself by implication as the Son of God in the parable of the wicked husbandmen (12:1–12), and more clearly in the discus-

5

sion about the Son of David. Finally, he acknowledges frankly before the Sanhedrin that he is the looked-for Messiah in the sense of the Son of man whom God will raise to his right hand (14:61f.). The road through the cross to glory which Jesus announces to his disciples at the beginning of this section and repeatedly recalls to them, three times in all, is described in a narrative which culminates in the confession of the pagan centurion at the foot of the cross (15:39) and the resurrection message at the tomb (16:6).

The listening Church, however, has not only to retrace its Lord's steps, it has to realize that it must actually follow and imitate him. Linked unmistakably with the first prediction of the Passion is a collection of sayings which call for cross-bearing, sacrifice, profession of faith in the Son of man, from all who wish to share in the glory of the coming kingdom of God (8:34—9:1). The second prediction of the Passion (9:30–32) is linked with a long passage of discourse addressed to the arguing disciples, which at the same time contains fundamental lessons for the Church in its earthly course (9:33–50). Similarly, the third and longest prophecy of Jesus' Passion (10:32–34) is followed by a warning to the sons of Zebedee that a cup of suffering and a baptism of death precede any share in Christ's glory, and by a lesson to all the disciples that the basic law of their community is not domination but service (10:35–45).

The Initiation of the Disciples into the Mystery of the Death of the Son of Man (8:31—10:45)

The first section consists of the three prophecies of the Passion (8:31; 9:31; 10:32ff.), and culminates in the statement that the Son is giving his life as a ransom for many (10:45). Then Jesus approaches the holy city of Jerusalem by way of Jericho, thus entering on the path that leads him to death. There is still time for a short period of ministry in Jerusalem, however, and this is taken up with some extremely significant controversies, rich in lessons for the Church in regard to its belief in Christ and its life in the world. Accordingly, another long section is devoted to this ministry in Jerusalem (10:46—13:37), while the last chapters recount the course of the Passion itself (14:1—16:8).

The evangelist himself by means of the triple prophecy of the Passion makes it quite plain that his aim is to initiate and lead us more and more deeply into the mystery of the death of the Son of man. An historically coherent, continuous narrative is therefore not to be expected in this section. The various elements are arranged by themes, and some of the larger units were perhaps taken over as they stand from tradition. It would be a mistake to inquire into the precise location or date of the transfiguration on the mountain. We can understand what this event must mean to anyone whose ears are ringing with the sayings about the Son of man having to suffer and the disciples having to take up the cross like him. We need not be surprised at the multiplicity and apparent lack of connection in Jesus' utterances during his private instruction of the disciples in the house at Capernaum (9:33–50). These are sayings of our Lord which were assembled at an early date under catchword headings, and important for the Church's life and organization. Consequently we must constantly bear in mind the particular theme under consideration, and subordinate all the themes to the guiding idea that we are following in the footsteps of the Lord as he goes to his death and overcomes the darkness of the world. And we are human beings who have to contend with human weakness and the temptations of our own heart, just like the disciples. Here, even more markedly than before, the disciples represent us as we too are summoned by the Lord.

The First Prediction of the Passion and Accompanying Passages (8:31—9:29)

JESUS' ANNOUNCEMENT OF THE PASSION AND PETER'S OPPOSITION (8:31–33)

[31]*And he began to teach them that the Son of man must suffer many things, and be rejected by the elders and the chief priests and the scribes, and be killed, and after three days rise again.* [32]*And he said this plainly. And Peter took him, and began to rebuke him.* [33]*But turning and seeing his disciples, he rebuked Peter, and said, " Get behind me, Satan! For you are not on the side of God, but of men."*

Jesus' announcement of the Passion is closely linked with Peter's confession that Jesus is the Messiah. In this way his prophecy of his death falls into place in the same question of who he is. Neither the multitude nor Peter has really grasped the mystery of Jesus. The spokesman of the group of disciples does indeed recognize Jesus' incomparable grandeur and confesses it with the highest attribute at his command, the messianic title of Messiah. But even this has false connotations. It can only become the full Christian confession of faith when the special nature of Jesus' messiahship and the path that has been laid down for him by God have been made plain. In this present teaching which is addressed in particular to the disciples (cf. 9:30), the twelve (10:32), and so to the Church, the very choice of another title marks the difference from Jewish expectations. Jesus speaks of the Son of man. He had already applied this term to himself before, in a mysteriously majestic sense, as exercising divine authority to forgive sins (2:10) and as lord of the sabbath (2:28). It is now said that this same Son of man must suffer and die. What is revealed here is the specifically Christian idea of the crucified and risen Messiah.

The whole prophecy of the rejection, Passion, and resurrection of the Son of man is expressed in the idiom of the early missionary preaching of the Church. Historically there is no reason to doubt that Jesus foresaw that suffering and death lay in store for him. The lack of comprehension shown by the people for his real mission, and the resistance of the ruling classes to his message and ministry were so patent that Jesus could have no doubt what the outcome of his earthly mission would be. It is impossible to say when he reached this certainty. The early Church was concerned with emphasizing Jesus' foreknowledge and resolute determination on his road to death and, even more, to make clear in the light of scripture the divine plan which lay behind it.

Closer examination of the prediction draws attention to the idea of " rejection." It is a harsh expression, implying more than judicial condemnation; the Son of man meets with scorn and contempt (9:12). And that is not all; there is probably a hidden scriptural reference. The same verb is used in a passage in a psalm which was of great importance for the early Church: " The stone which the builders rejected has become the head of the corner; this is the Lord's doing, and it is marvelous in our eyes " (Ps. 118:22f.). The passage is quoted in connection with the parable of the wicked husbandmen (Mk. 12:10f.), which plainly refers to the killing of Jesus. As the early Church understood it, the Jewish leaders had rejected God's final envoy, the Son of God, but God had confirmed him and made him the foundation of salvation. The builders are the men who ought to have recognized the importance of the stone.

The resurrection prophecy is included in all three predictions of the Passion; it is remarkable, however, that in each case the disciples pay no special attention to it. A psychological explanation, that they were so frightened and bewildered by what was said about the sufferings and death of the Son of man that they did not notice the promise, is out of place. The resurrection is part of God's saving plan and has to be included in this keryg-matic formula. It is worded more by reference to the scriptural background than to the resurrection event. In contrast to the text of I Corinthians 15:4, it does not say "was raised" but "rise again," and not "on the third day" but "after three days." Of course these verbal variations are of little importance, since the thought is the same: it is God who in a very short time, after three days or on the third day, causes the man who has been killed to rise to life again. "Three days" is a frequent expression in the Old Testament and in Judaism for a short period of suffering and trial followed by a turning point, help and deliverance by God. ". . . the Lord . . . has torn, that he may heal us; he has stricken, and he will bind us up. After two days he will revive us; on the third day he will raise us up, that we may live before him" (Hos. 6:1f.). The early Church also applied other sayings concerning "three days" to Jesus' resur-rection.

Jesus now speaks to the disciples " plainly "—openly and con-fidently—about his road to suffering and death. That is the turning point that had been reached at Caesarea Philippi; until then Jesus had kept his secret to himself. The disciples had not understood his messianic ministry (cf. 6:52; 8:17–21) and now they have no idea where Jesus' way will lead him. But if their faith is not to collapse, their eyes must be opened to the neces-sity of the Passion and death of their Lord. And that applies not only to them as they were at that moment, but also to the com-munity later, which felt Jesus' shameful death to be harsh and incomprehensible. The divine meaning of this event has to be fully manifested in retrospect. In the mirror of the teaching given to the disciples, the Church recognizes its own resistance, and Jesus' threefold clear prophecy is intended to lead it deeply and securely into God's thoughts.

The same disciple who had made the confession of faith in

Jesus' messiahship in the name of the others becomes Jesus' adversary and tempter. He takes him aside and starts to remonstrate with him. It is a duel between Peter and Jesus, as the use of the same verb shows: Peter roundly "rebukes" the Lord for thinking of sufferings and death, and Jesus "rebukes" the leading disciple just as decidedly. In view of all the disciples—Jesus turns and "sees his disciples"—Jesus rejects as a diabolical temptation Peter's demand that he should desist from taking his road to death. The harshness of this rebuff is striking. The words "Get behind me, Satan!" are also found at the end of Matthew's account of the temptation in the desert, and were perhaps taken by Matthew from the incident with Peter. But Mark himself, who on both occasions uses the term "Satan" (not "devil"), recognized the similarity between the temptation in the desert and Peter's adjuration: Jesus was to be led astray into a political messiahship, to a striving for earthly power and dominion in contradiction to God's plan. It is the most dangerous temptation, which perpetually befalls human beings (cf. Mk. 10:37, 42), and has to be overcome by obedience to God's call. Even Mark's community seems not yet to have come to terms with a suffering and dying Messiah, and seems to have dreamt of an earthly realm. The Church is not called to political dominion; its ministry in the world is to bear testimony to love and the will to peace (cf. 9:50); its earthly lot is to imitate the crucified Lord. Jesus says sternly, "You do not think the thoughts of God, but those of men." The present-day attitude of openness to the world, the Christian's commitment in the world, comes up against a limit here. The saving mission of the whole Church is not a political one, and the individual Christian who has to act in various earthly domains can never deny his Lord's way of the cross. He too must obey God rather than men and, if circumstances demand it, must accept abuse and suffering for himself.

DISCIPLESHIP IN SUFFERING AND DEATH (8:34—9:1)

³⁴*And he called to him the multitude with his disciples, and said to them, " If any man would come after me, let him deny himself and take up his cross and follow me. ³⁵For whoever would save his life will lose it; and whoever loses his life for my sake and the gospel's will save it. ³⁶For what does it profit a man to gain the whole world and forfeit his life? ³⁷For what can a man give in return for his life? ³⁸For whoever is ashamed of me and of my words in this adulterous and sinful generation, of him will the Son of man also be ashamed when he comes in the glory of his Father with the holy angels." ¹And he said to them, " Truly, I say to you, there are some standing here who will not taste death before they see the kingdom of God come with power."*

The collection of sayings which follow is addressed to the whole community. The " multitude " which cannot be at hand in these circumstances (Matthew and Luke omit it) represents all who are to hear Jesus' message. The disciples are expressly mentioned in order to address the faithful (probably not leaders in the Church specifically). This is also shown by the phrase " called to him," which Mark uses in order to impart important lessons to the multitude or the disciples, and through them to later believers (cf. 7 : 14; 10 : 42; 12 : 43). In this way Jesus' sayings, which have been put together from early tradition, become a lasting call to all men; they have to come to see the way of the Son of man as something that concerns themselves. What Jesus says about his sufferings and death is not intended only to throw light on the darkness of his own lot but also to point out the way the disciples are to follow and imitate. The second and third sayings about gaining and losing " life " sound like an interpretation of human existence generally, like wisdom sayings expressing the paradoxical, contradictory element in human experience.

But inserted as they are between the classical saying about bearing one's cross and that on confessing the Son of man, they too are a summons to cope with life as a disciple of Christ. Suffering and death are inescapable in earthly existence, but by imitation of Jesus they can be overcome, because they lead to the depth and fullness of a life to which man secretly aspires.

The saying about taking up the cross has been quoted so often that it has lost its edge, but in reality it is an extremely harsh saying, similar to the *agraphon* (a saying of our Lord not handed down in the gospels): " He who is near me is near fire; he who is far from me is far from the kingdom." Jesus in fact spoke in such a forbidding way in order to make clear the seriousness and grandeur of the discipleship he demands (cf. Lk. 9:57f.; 14:25–35). His invitation to follow him is for courageous human beings who decide to do so with full realization of the steepness of the way and in complete liberty, because the goal is worth the effort. In its original sense, the saying is a call to imitation ("come after me") which seems to end in disgrace and death. " To take up one's cross " in the literal sense could only mean for a person of that time: to set off on the terrible path of a man condemned to death by crucifixion, carrying on his shoulders the heavy beam to which he will be nailed, lifted up, and pilloried at the place of execution. This sight was familiar to the people at that time, and therefore the metaphor means " to venture on a life which is as difficult as the last walk of a man condemned to death." A different interpretation has indeed been suggested; " cross " would refer to the Hebrew letter *tau* or a Greek *tau*, which resembled a cross. In the Old Testament and later symbolism this could be a sign of divine protection, a mark of divine ownership, which also demanded of its bearer a radical dedication to the divine will. Thus we read in a prophecy of Ezekiel, " Go through the city, through Jerusalem, and put a mark (tau) upon the foreheads of the men who sigh and groan

over all the abominations that are committed in it" (Ezek.
9:4ff.). The meaning of Jesus' words would accordingly be:
Take God's sign on yourself as a sign of radical selfgiving to
God! This is a profound meaning, not at all remote from the
mind of Jesus, a symbolic interpretation which was certainly
possible among Jews at that time, but Jesus would surely have
expressed it more clearly. He is not referring to his way to the
cross, which is not even mentioned in the predictions of the
Passion; it was only after the cross and resurrection that the
Christians could have that thought in their minds.

The saying about saving and losing life (verse 35) takes its
edge from the key word of "life." The word in Greek means
"soul," but in the Old Testament it means more than this: the
whole living human being, with his will to life, the expressions
of his life, his whole existence as a human person. He who
wants to develop his own ego and save his personal existence for
himself will lose his life and hopelessly miss life's goal. But he
who thinks little of his earthly life and sacrifices it in following
Jesus, will save his life, attain its true goal. The saying is often
explained as though the word "life" were used in a double
sense of earthly, natural life and eternal life with God. That is
not incorrect, but blunts the sharp edge of the paradoxical
saying, for the same expression is in fact used each time. The
word *psyche* receives no second sense, but is, rather, opened out,
transcended. It is no longer used absolutely, in the sense of
man's earthly existence. This existence stands in a different
frame of reference—behind the present and future which will
end one day, stands a definitive future.

The next saying (v. 36f.) amounts to the same thing but also
shows more clearly the fragility of a purely "worldly" existence. It is foolish and pointless to accumulate this world's goods,
to pursue material gain only to forfeit authentically human existence, personal fulfillment and life in the spiritual source and

ground of all life, in God. The well-known translation " and
suffer the loss of his own soul " blunts the edge of the saying
because it is a question of man's very being or non-being. Of
course it is not merely a matter of human prudence—of what
use are wealth and prosperity to a man since he must die. What
is at stake is the ultimate in human existence, which is either
gained or missed at bodily death: eternal life with God. The
idea is best illustrated by the parable of the rich fool (Lk.
12:16–21). The folly of that rich man, who relied on his possessions and told his " soul " to take its ease and enjoy life,
was not that he had to leave it all to his delighted heirs, but that
he laid up treasure for himself and not with God. God will
have no regard for him and will let him come to nothing,
requiring his " life " of him in the terrible sense that there will
no longer be any future for him.

The whole series of sayings is concluded by a difficult logion
which represents the coming of the kingdom of God in power
as immediately imminent. Its location here is certainly due to
the fact that mention has just been made of the parousia. But
the evangelist has also made it stand out from the series of sayings by an introductory formula of his own which he often uses
(" And he said to them "). In fact it is intended rather as a con-
soling prophecy, in contrast to the threatened judgment of
8:38. For the Church, Jesus' coming in power means salvation
from affliction and distress (cf. 13:27). For a long time now it
has been disputed whether it is an authentic saying of Jesus
himself, one of his sayings applied to the situation of the community, or a community formation, perhaps based on an utterance of primitive Christian prophecy. There is a clearly recognizable expectation that the second coming is imminent; the
community expects the parousia for the present generation (cf.
13:30), when some of the witnesses of Jesus' earthly ministry are
still alive. An old-fashioned expression is used: some of those

listening to Jesus' words (those "standing here") will "not taste death" until they experience the coming of the kingdom of God with power.

JESUS' TRANSFIGURATION (9:2-8)

2And after six days Jesus took with him Peter and James and John, and led them up a high mountain apart by themselves; and he was transfigured before them, 3and his garments became glistening, intensely white, as no fuller on earth could bleach them. 4And there appeared to them Elijah with Moses; and they were talking to Jesus. 5And Peter said to Jesus, " Master, it is well that we are here; let us make three booths, one for you and one for Moses and one for Elijah." 6For he did not know what to say, for they were exceedingly afraid. 7And a cloud overshadowed them, and a voice came out of the cloud, " This is my beloved Son; listen to him." 8And suddenly looking around they no longer saw anyone with them but Jesus only.

Jesus' transfiguration on a high mountain, like the events after Jesus' baptism and his walking on the lake, is a theophany story, and as such is inaccessible to the historian's critical investigation; it discloses its meaning only to faith. But the wealth of themes and of their possible combinations make it very difficult to determine with any precision even what its meaning is for faith. The story of Jesus' transfiguration was undoubtedly current in the post-paschal Church, before Mark, who took it and incorporated it in his gospel with definite intentions in mind.

The time and place of the occurrence are not stated, though the precise notations " after six days " and " a high mountain " might seem to do so. These " six days " cannot be reckoned from the conversation at Caesarea Philippi, because between the two there is that calling together of the multitude and his disciples (8:34), the duration of which it is impossible to determine. Mount Tabor in Galilee, traditionally venerated as the mountain of the transfiguration, is certainly a magnificent site on which even today the theophanic event can readily be imagined, the manifestation of the world of God within earthly reality.

Two heavenly figures appear, "Elijah with Moses," men of God of the Old Testament, rich in associations for Judaism. What is their significance in this scene? Are they only there in attendance, to make the theophanic occasion more impressive? Angels would have served equally well; the two men of God have been deliberately chosen. Are they there to bear witness to Jesus? They speak to him, not to the disciples. Their testimony consists simply in their presence and their personal significance. Do they symbolize the Law and the Prophets, as has often been thought? Yet Elijah was not a writing prophet, and the order chosen by Mark (and only by him) also tells against that. Do they figure as forerunners of the Messiah? It is true that Elijah was viewed in this light (cf. vv. 11f.), but it is doubtful whether Judaism at that time attributed such a role to Moses. Are they named as men of God who were taken up to God without bodily death? Judaism attributed to Moses an assumption into heaven of this kind, which the Old Testament attests in the case of Enoch and Elijah. They speak with Jesus, thus showing their fellowship with him, and this could mean that Jesus too will be one of their number. Of course he is not taken up as they were without bodily death, but is raised from the dead. What is certain is that they are meant to point to Jesus as the greater, the one who is awaited, who fulfills all hopes.

In the meantime, however, there is an intervention by Peter. This disciple is so fascinated by the wonderful scene that he wants to build three booths, one for Jesus, one for Moses and one for Elijah. He would like to invite these radiant figures to remain, because he wants to cling to the happiness of this moment and contribute what he can to it, with his companions. The three " tents " recall the Feast of Tabernacles, which was associated with strong messianic and eschatological expectations; the festival week was an anticipation of the rejoicing of the era of salvation. Peter does not want to build the booths for himself and the two other disciples, but for Jesus and the heavenly figures. It is the counterpart to his attitude after Jesus' prophecy of his death (8: 32). There he adjured Jesus to desist from that course and purpose. Here he attempts to induce the radiant figures to stay. Mark regards this as inappropriate, but explains it by the holy awe which had gripped the disciples.

At this point God himself intervenes. The cloud which overshadowed them, that is, probably, the disciples, is the sign of the divine presence (cf. Ex. 24: 15–18), a saving presence, which is at once revelation, promise, and admonition. The voice of God (cf. the commentary on 1: 11) reveals Jesus as his beloved Son, greater than Elijah, more than Moses, different from the expected Messiah. In contrast to the voice at the baptism, the words this time are addressed not to Jesus but to the disciples, and for them the significant clause is added: " Listen to him." The very words recall the promise of a prophet who was one day to come, like Moses: " The Lord your God will raise up for you a prophet like me from among you, from your brethren—him you shall heed! " (Deut. 18: 15). This admonition is even more strongly emphasized a little further on: " And whoever will not give heed to my words which he shall speak in my name, I myself will require it of him " (18: 19). The allusion to the prophet-Messiah promised by Moses himself also adds a new emphasis to Moses' presence here. For the evangelist, however, this admonition has a very concrete meaning. Even the perplexing things which Jesus had said to his disciples about his road to death and their need to follow him on it, are presented to the disciples and to the later Church as God's words, which impose a duty of obedience.

Thereupon the heavenly scene disappears. The disciples look around and see no one but Jesus with his ordinary appearance, similar to themselves once again. This abrupt cessation of the phenomenon after the divine voice, also has a deep meaning. The purpose of the revelation has been achieved, God's admonition rings out: Listen to him! The whole thing was just like the heavens opening after Jesus' baptism, a ray of light from on high, momentarily piercing earthly darkness. The harsh reality of earth remains. It is not yet the time of fulfillment and glory: the way of suffering and death has to be trodden first. Together with the disciples, the Church is taught that the Son of man must suffer many things, be rejected, and put to death. The only gleam of silver on the horizon is the promise that after three days he will rise again. He is God's beloved Son, and he will not remain in death but is called to heavenly glory, to the attainment of his goal with God.

What, then, is the significance of this numinous narrative for Mark? It is the incipient disclosure of Jesus' messianic secret, manifestation of his hidden glory despite his imminent death, and, even more, vindication of Jesus' way of death and divine authentication of his words. All this constitutes an admonition to the Church not to give way at the thought of Jesus' cross but to follow in his footsteps. The three disciples are the chosen witnesses of this revelation, just as they are the witnesses of Jesus' agony on the Mount of Olives (14:33f.). And just as the series of sayings about following Jesus to death is concluded by the promise of the coming of the Son of man in glory (8:38), and of the coming of the kingdom of God with power (9:1), so too the transfiguration on the mountain confirms that promise. It opens out the prospect of Jesus' vindication and installation in power by God, without annulling the prophecy of his Passion and death. That is why this narrative stands in the course of Jesus' earthly life is strong contrast to his prophecy of his death.

CONVERSATION DURING THE DESCENT FROM THE MOUNTAIN OF THE TRANSFIGURATION (9: 9–13)

And as they were coming down the mountain, he charged them to tell no one what they had seen, until the Son of man should have risen from the dead. ¹⁰So they kept the matter to themselves, questioning what the rising from the dead meant. ¹¹And they asked him, " Why do the scribes say that first Elijah must come? " ¹²And he said to them, " Elijah does come first to restore all things; and how is it written of the Son of man, that he should suffer many things and be treated with contempt? ¹³But I tell you that Elijah has come, and they did to him whatever they pleased, as it is written of him."

The conversation that Jesus holds with the three disciples as they come down the mountain bears stronger marks of editorial handling than the transfiguration pericope itself, and consequently allows us to see more deeply into the evangelist's intentions. The subject matter does not directly concern the theophany on the mountain but is more closely linked with 8:31. The statement in Jesus' prediction of his death which the disciples had seemed to have overlooked, namely, that the Son of man will rise again after three days, now becomes the focus of attention. Jesus' command to them to be silent " until the Son of man should have risen from the dead " (9:9) refers to this, and prompts the disciples first of all to consider what rising from the dead means. Then, however, they raise an objection which returns once again to the need for the sufferings and humiliation of the Son of man. The reference to the Jewish expectation that Elijah is to come first was probably suggested to the evangelist by the appearance of Elijah at the transfiguration.

The command to the three disciples to keep silence (Luke does not include it) is hard to understand in the historical situation, like similar earlier commands. If the disciples and others who had heard Jesus' prediction of his death were to receive light on this obscure fact and thereby be encouraged to follow him in his sufferings, why should the three witnesses of Jesus' transfiguration not be allowed to speak about it, at least to their fellow disciples? However, the reference to the resurrection is important to the evangelist for several reasons. Jesus' transfiguration points ahead to his resurrection and becomes really intelligible only through it. The choice of these particular three disciples as witnesses of the raising to life of the daughter of Jairus (5:37), of the transfiguration, and of the agony in the garden (14:33), is relevant to mysteries of Jesus' earthly life and ministry which must not remain hidden after his resurrection, for they provide a key to the understanding of his person. The hidden agent is, after all, the Son of God endowed with full authority and destined to have God's glory and power, even though he must pass through the dark night of suffering. At least three of the oldest and closest companions of Jesus are to testify to this later, when it has become comprehensible to the Church as a result of Jesus' resurrection. Even at this moment, when the disciples are coming down from the mountain of the transfiguration, Jesus' words about the resurrection of the Son of man are still incomprehensible to them. They do indeed seize on this saying, but dispute about the meaning of resurrection from the dead. " From the dead " is probably used deliberately in contrast to 8:31 in order to express even more forcefully Jesus' real entry into the realm of the dead and his God-effected emergence from it, his rising up again. It is the eschatological hope of Judaism for the end of the ages, which in fact was to be fulfilled in Jesus soon after death. This was the tremendous, overwhelming experience of the group of disciples, and what fired their Easter faith and joy. When it actually happened and the disciples could know it by the appearances of the risen Christ (confirmed by the empty tomb), then " rising from the dead," to be awakened from death by God's power, was the formula which suggested itself to them as making the event comprehensible and disclosing its full significance. The resurrection is God's sign that he confirms and vindicates Jesus the crucified, causes the definitive era of salvation to dawn in him, brings history to its accomplishment, and gives men the certainty of their own deliverance.

After the discussion among themselves, the three disciples come and question Jesus. The Jewish scribes said that according to scripture Elijah had first to come. What is the force of this argument if Jesus talks of the resurrection of the Son of man and makes no mention of Elijah's coming? The disciples have obviously understood—here the post-paschal outlook is evident—that the statement concerns the eschatological time of salvation. Jesus first confirms the Jewish view based on scripture. One would have expected him to go on at once: " But I say to you that Elijah has already come " (that is how Matthew sets out the sequence of ideas). Mark, however, immediately after Jesus' confirmation of the Jewish hope, abruptly raises the objection: How can it then be written that the Son of man must suffer many things and be treated with contempt? He expresses the difficulties felt by the Christian community, which is holding fast to Jesus' own statement (8:31). The community then hears the answer from Jesus' own lips: Elijah has come and men did to him whatever they pleased.

It is clear (and Matthew makes it even clearer by an explanatory remark of his own, 17:13) that John the Baptist is meant. For the Christians he was truly the forerunner of Jesus the

Messiah and could accordingly be viewed in the role which Judaism assigned to Elijah on his return.

CURE OF THE EPILEPTIC DEMONIAC; THE NECESSITY OF FAITH (9:14-29)

[14]*And when they came to the disciples, they saw a great crowd about them, and scribes arguing with them.* [15]*And immediately all the crowd, when they saw him, were greatly amazed, and ran up to him and greeted him.* [16]*And he asked them, " What are you discussing with them?"* [17]*And one of the crowd answered him, " Teacher, I brought my son to you, for he has a dumb spirit;* [18]*and wherever it seizes him, it dashes him down; and he foams and grinds his teeth and becomes rigid; and I asked your disciples to cast it out, and they were not able."* [19]*And he answered them, " O faithless generation, how long am I to be with you? How long am I to bear with you? Bring him to me."* [20]*And they brought the boy to him; and when the spirit saw him, immediately it convulsed the boy, and he fell on the ground and rolled about, foaming at the mouth.* [21]*And Jesus asked his father, " How long has he had this?" And he said, " From childhood.* [22]*And it has often cast him into the fire and into the water, to destroy him; but if you can do anything, have pity on us and help us."* [23]*And Jesus said to him, " If you can! All things are possible to him who believes."* [24]*Immediately the father of the child cried out and said, " I believe; help my un-belief!"* [25]*And when Jesus saw that a crowd came running to-gether, he rebuked the unclean spirit, saying to it, " You dumb and deaf spirit, I command you, come out of him, and never enter him again."* [26]*And after crying out and convulsing him terribly, it came out, and the boy was like a corpse; so that most of them said, " He is dead."* [27]*But Jesus took him by the hand*

and lifted him up, and he arose. [28]*And when he had entered the house, his disciples asked him privately, "Why could we not cast it out?"* [29]*And he said to them, "This kind cannot be driven out by anything but prayer."*

As they come down from the mountain, they find a big crowd of people and scribes arguing with other disciples—a very different scene. It is not said what the argument was about; probably the scribes are only mentioned because a discussion is involved. From what follows it seems probable they were talking about the power to cast out evil spirits, and whether Jesus himself could cure this serious case of possession. The father had wanted to bring his unfortunate son to Jesus but had found only the disciples, who were unable to do anything about the illness. The crowd was waiting for Jesus, but when they saw him they " were greatly amazed."

The father describes his son's affliction; he is possessed by an evil spirit which seizes him suddenly and throws him on the ground. The description of the boy's foaming and grinding his teeth and then lying exhausted or rigid, suggests an epileptic fit. The spirit is probably called " dumb " (and also, v. 25, " deaf ") because the boy had great difficulty in speaking; the symptoms of the patient's illness were all attributed to the evil spirit. Concerned as people were in those days about such horrible phenomena, the point at issue here is the possibility of casting out the evil spirit, that is, of a cure. The disciples were helpless, and Jesus is reproached with this.

Jesus blames the " faithless generation," an expression which recalls his answer to the unbelieving Jews who called for a sign: " An evil and adulterous generation seeks for a sign " (Mt. 12 : 39 par. Lk. 11 : 29). Jesus condemns the attitude of the crowd as a mere desire to see miracles, a purely superficial attachment for the sake of help in earthly troubles.

Yet Jesus, when confronted with human narrowness of heart and obstinacy, does not allow himself to be resigned to it, but remains faithful to God's mandate to proclaim and minister to salvation. It is only a human sigh, as it were, that is forced from his heart; these people pain him, but he turns to them at once in love and mercy. A stimulus to preachers and all the faithful not to capitulate before the resistance met with in the world around them or in their own hearts. Jesus has the boy brought to him, and the boy has a fit before his very eyes. Jesus' question as to how long the boy has been afflicted like this gives the father an opportunity to describe more fully the gravity of the case. His son has had epileptic attacks since childhood, and they have often made him run into water or fire to the danger of his life. On that account, Matthew diagnosed the illness as lunacy. Mark, however, sees in this the malice of the demon seeking to kill the child. Against the destructive force of evil, only strong faith can prevail.

After the lament over the unbelieving generation, faith becomes the theme. Jesus answers the words of the despairing father, " If you can do anything," with the admonition that " All things are possible to him who believes." The man's request implies a doubt about Jesus' power to free the boy from his affliction. Jesus' answer therefore seems to mean that he himself will undertake the exorcism by the power of faith.

When Jesus saw how people kept on arriving and swelling the crowd, he at once began the exorcism. He clearly wanted to avoid causing any further stir. The events described resemble those of a previous occasion. The devil cannot but obey the mighty command, but leaves unwillingly with a loud cry, and a final convulsion of the boy. The result is noted. The patient lies completely exhausted as though dead. The reaction of the crowd is characteristic. Most of them say the boy is dead. There is no praise and astonishment at the mighty deed (cf. 1:27). This unfavorable reaction is certainly intended by the evangelist. The crowd was not made any more believing by this astounding exorcism, which must have been even more impressive after the disciples' failure; they remain an unbelieving generation. For believing readers, however, Jesus' action is a confirmation of his majesty and power. Jesus' command is marked by an emphatic " I." Unlike the disciples, he commands the unclean spirit with sovereign authority to go and not to return. When the demon has departed, Jesus takes the hand of the apparently lifeless boy, just as he did with the daughter of Jairus, whom he had awakened from the sleep of death (5:41), and lifts him up. Then it is said that " he arose," just as was said of the dead girl (5:42). The evangelist obviously wished to liken this cure to a raising from the dead, and for the attentive reader it is a pointer to Jesus' power over the force of death.

The ensuing conversation between the disciples and Jesus clearly shows that the evangelist wishes to convey another special lesson to the Church. The " house " and the " privately " are stylistic devices used by the evangelist to draw the Church's attention to Jesus' answer, which concludes the whole narrative (cf. 4:34; 7:17; 9:33; 10:10f.; 13:3f.). The disciples ask why they were not able to heal the demoniac boy, and Jesus tells them, " This kind cannot be driven out by anything but prayer." Since the readers have heard nothing about any prayer on Jesus' part, this answer is obviously addressed to the Church. To faith, to which all things are possible, must be added prayer, calling on God's power, not of course in order to have it at command, but in the sense of humble petition, looking to God in faith for what is humanly impossible. Such prayer shows what true faith really is.

The Second Prediction of the Passion and a Collection of Sayings for the Church (9 : 30–50)

The repeated prediction of Jesus' Passion and death marks a new section which is even more clearly addressed to the Church. The conversation with the disciples "in the house" (9:33) forms the framework of a sort of Church catechism, comprising various sayings of Jesus all concerning the Church. The various brief items are linked by catchwords, an early device for remembering and transmitting Jesus' sayings. This distinctive and, in substance, probably pre-Marcan catchword composition, 9:30–50, shows how the Church "remembered the words of the Lord" (cf. Acts 20:35) and applied them to its own situation.

THE SECOND PREDICTION OF THE PASSION (9:30–32)

³⁰*They went on from there and passed through Galilee. And he would not have anyone know it;* ³¹*for he was teaching his disciples, saying to them, " The Son of man will be delivered into the hands of men, and they will kill him; and when he is killed, after three days he will rise."* ³²*But they did not understand the saying, and they were afraid to ask him.*

The evangelist's introductory sentence is intended to serve as transition from the items just narrated to new materials from tradition, and at the same time to announce Jesus' departure for Jerusalem. For in the chapters which follow he systematically strengthens the impression that Jesus is making his way on foot to the holy city. After 10:1 he arrives in the region of Judea and east of the Jordan; after 10:7 he sets off again; in 10:32 the destination is expressly said to be Jerusalem; in 10:46 he reaches

Jericho; in 11:1 he is approaching the capital via Bethphage and Bethany; finally he enters Jerusalem and goes into the temple (11:11). The geographical indications are imprecise; some are obscure and misleading. Some items, such as the teaching of the crowds in 10:1, the discussion with the Pharisees in 10:2ff., the blessing of the children in 10:13ff., do not fit this framework, and the change of audience (crowd, disciples) confirms that the pericopes have probably been assembled for theological purposes because of their content. The journey to Jerusalem has theological significance because the destiny of death ordained for him by God is to be fulfilled there. The disciples are taken with him on this way. Jesus " walks ahead of them " (10:32), and the Church is to know that all this is addressed to it too by its Lord on his way to the cross. This lends to his words profound seriousness, especially as the Church must recognize its own image in the disciples' failure to understand and the way they run counter to Jesus' spirit. Luke places this journey of Jesus to Jerusalem, undertaken with full awareness and holy determination (Lk. 9:51), in even higher relief, with theological emphasis especially on the idea that the destiny of the prophets was fulfilled in Jerusalem and so must that of the Messiah (cf. 13:32-35). Mark, in the present passage, describes Jesus' passing through Galilee, the home of the gospel and the scene of his mighty deeds, without stopping and as far as possible unrecognized and unnoticed. It is his final departure from the scenes of his ministry, the abrupt end of his proclamation of salvation, because the hour has struck for the Son of man to be delivered up to death. " And he would not have anyone know it." No one must hinder Jesus, or hold him back. In contrast to the earlier demand for silence, we now hear no mention of his intention becoming known.

In comparison with the first prediction of the Passion, we notice that the " must " which expresses the divine ordinance is not included. Instead, it is expressly said that " He will be delivered." The mysterious event has become a fact, it is already beginning to take place. Jesus has consented, and is setting off without delay. But the humanly incomprehensible mystery persists, grievous and crushing. The Son of man will be "delivered into the hands of men." In 8 : 31 it had been said that he was to be rejected by the elders, chief priests, and scribes, in other words, by the theocratic officials of Judaism. The expression now is even more fundamental: the Son of man who is called by God to glory (8 : 38) will be delivered into the hands of men.

Yet once again the disciples are quite devoid of understanding. They no longer contradict him, they do not even dare question him, they are shy and afraid of him. What he says—the whole statement about men killing him, and the resurrection—is so great and incomprehensible that awe overwhelms them as it did after the calming of the storm (4 : 41). Jesus' words are unimpeachable, irresistible like those regarding Peter's denial, which the disciple remembered bitterly after his fall (14 : 72). The Church is to realize that Jesus said it, endorsed God's decision, and made known God's design. According to this saying, Jesus' death is an indelible reminder of the wickedness of men, but also of the power of God.

THE DISCIPLES' DISPUTE OVER PRECEDENCE (9 : 33-37)

[33]*And they came to Capernaum; and when he was in the house he asked them, " What were you discussing on the way?"* [34]*But they were silent; for on the way they had discussed with one another who was the greatest.* [35]*And he sat down and called the twelve; and he said to them, " If anyone would be first, he must be last of all and servant of all."* [36]*And he took a child, and put him in the midst of them; and taking him in his arms, he said to them,* [37]*" Whoever receives one such child in my name receives*

*me; and whoever receives me, receives not me but him who
sent me."*

Despite the departure for Jerusalem (cf. v. 30), we find ourselves
once more in Capernaum, in the north of Galilee. The evangelist
has composed this setting for his collection of sayings because
Capernaum was the town where Jesus was " at home " (cf. 2 : 1),
that is, in the house of Simon and Andrew (1 : 29). That is the
idea here also. On the journey resolutely begun towards the place
of his Passion and death, Jesus calls in " at home " once more
and gives the disciples further important lessons. The Church
knows that these words of Jesus to the twelve are addressed to
it too. On the way, when Jesus' thoughts were wholly occupied
with his Passion, the disciples had been discussing which of them
was the greatest. They were so far from him, they had so little
realization of what it means to follow Jesus. It is exactly the
same contrast as between Jesus' first prediction of the Passion
and Peter's remonstrance (8 : 31ff.). All the disciples are entangled in human thoughts; they are even arguing about who is
to have the first place. But Jesus—the evangelist shows this by
the question to the disciples—knows them, and they are silent
in embarrassment. The next observation, that he sat down—the
posture of the teacher (cf. 4 : 1f.; 13 : 3)—and called the twelve to
him, comes from the pen of the evangelist. It shows that he has
something special to say to them (cf. 6 : 7), the representatives
of the people of God (3 : 13ff.). The " twelve " will be mentioned
several times as accompanying him on the way to death (10 : 32;
11 : 11; 14 : 17). Jesus wishes to take them—and with them the
Church—with him along this path, in mind and soul as well.
This constitutes the setting for the words which follow and
which the evangelist drew from tradition.

The saying that the disciple who is ambitious to excel must be
last and the servant of all, has been handed down in the gospels

in five versions, so important was it to the primitive Church. The demand which Jesus thus makes on all who wish to belong to the community of his disciples and to himself, assails the deeply rooted human urge to self-assertion and ambition, and subverts the state of affairs that prevails in worldly spheres (cf. 10:42). Jesus spoke in provocative terms of this kind, not to start a revolution against earthly rulers (which would only bring others to power anyway), but in order to create a new order, mirroring God's rule and foreshadowing his coming kingdom. For God " rules " by his merciful love, and Jesus exercises his God-given power by service. The community of disciples and the future Church are thus placed under a new " law " which appears to contradict every law of human society yet alone brings true deliverance in the ceaseless human struggle for existence, in the clash of pressure groups and the competition for leadership and power. In earthly institutions, State, and society, such an order cannot of course be achieved at all, or only imperfectly. With the best will in the world, rulers as " first servants of the State " and " ministers " as responsible representatives of the people, cannot discharge their office in the radical way of service that Jesus' words to his disciples imply.

Jesus brings a child in the midst of the disciples, putting his arms round the child and caressing him, as Mark also says in the other scene with children, where they are given a blessing (10:16). It is evident that the evangelist himself assimilated these scenes to one another. Tradition gave him various sayings about children, and he fitted these into various scenes as he thought most appropriate. In the present context as composed by Mark, in which a child is placed in front of the disciples, not as in Matthew as a sign of smallness and humility (18:3f.), but as an object of their care, the saying takes on another meaning. Jesus loves and embraces such a child and takes his part, as though wanting to impress on the disciples who are striving for precedence, that if they wish to belong to him they must respect the small and insignificant, for in such a child it is Jesus they meet. Jesus is a friend of the insignificant, despised people of whom the child is a symbol. Jesus would thus indirectly be pointing to his own example, his own attitude and disposition (as in 10:45).

THE STRANGE EXORCIST AND A FURTHER SAYING (9:38–41)

[38]John said to him, " Teacher, we saw a man casting out demons in your name, and we forbade him, because he was not following us." [39]But Jesus said, " Do not forbid him; for no one who does a mighty work in my name will be able soon after to speak evil of me. [40]For he that is not against us is for us. [41]For truly, I say to you, whoever gives you a cup of water to drink because you bear the name of Christ, will by no means lose his reward.

With the " strange exorcist," Mark exhibits a special tradition. John, the son of Zebedee, is not mentioned by chance or without reason. In a specifically Lucan tradition, he and his brother James appear in an equally impatient fashion, wanting to call down fire from heaven on a Samaritan village which refused to offer hospitality to Jesus and his disciples (Lk. 9:54f.). The incident that John reports is not inconceivable in Jesus' time. We hear from other sources of Jewish exorcists who employed various magical practices. But a concern of the Church can also quite clearly be discerned. We learn from Acts that the Samaritan Simon Magus tried to purchase the power of miracles from the apostle Peter (Acts 8:18f.). A magical mode of thought of that kind was widespread in that age and may also have persisted in the margin of the early communities. The remark that the strange exorcist did not follow " us " is noteworthy, for elsewhere in the gospels only following Jesus is mentioned. Consequently the Church will have contemporary events in mind. But the lesson which Jesus gives the disciples is in accordance with his spirit, just as the rebuke is in Luke 9:55. It is an expression of patience and generosity, which provided a guideline for the Christian Church.

The reason Jesus gives seems at first sight an opportunistic one —anyone who acquires something of Jesus' power will not easily be in a position to revile him. Jesus seems to be aiming at collecting adherents and friends. But this " rational " argument (which Luke omits) is simply intended to make the disciples realize the folly of their behavior. It culminates in a saying which was of special interest for the Church: " He that is not against me is for me." These are tolerant words, redolent of a breadth of mind above narrow party spirit.

Who is the person who is promised a reward even for a cup of water offered to Jesus' disciples? For Mark and his Church in this context it can only mean an outsider who is not hostile to Christ and his followers, for he performs this service for Christ's sake. Mark (or an early copyist) clarified this by adding the phrase " because you belong to Christ " (Jesus cannot have said this); but the old Semitic construction " in the name, that " (as the Greek text runs) points to an early saying which Jesus may, for example, have spoken when sending his disciples on the mission (cf. Mk. 6:7–13; Lk. 10:5–11). The early Church applied it to its missionary situation, for which Matthew too uses it, in his own way (10:42). It is a saying which envisages difficulties the disciples will encounter, but which should also reassure them. There are kind people who help others out of common humanity even though they are not professed Christians; they will experience God's mercy at the Judgment. As with the good

Samaritan and the description of the Judgment, Jesus praises a humanitarianism which sometimes puts Christians to shame. These are the people he is referring to when he says, " He that is not against us is for us."

OCCASIONS OF SIN (9:42–48)

[42] " *Whoever causes one of these little ones who believe in me to sin, it would be better for him if a great millstone were hung round his neck and he were thrown into the sea.* [43]*And if your hand causes you to sin, cut it off; it is better for you to enter life maimed than with two hands to go to hell, to the unquenchable fire.* [45]*And if your foot causes you to sin, cut it off; it is better for you to enter life lame than with two feet to be thrown into hell.* [47]*And if your eye causes you to sin, pluck it out; it is better for you to enter the kingdom of God with one eye than with two eyes to be thrown into hell,* [48]*where their worm does not die, and the fire is not quenched.*

This new set of sayings is linked with the catchword " cause of sin " (" scandal "). It is joined to what precedes by the catchword " little ones "; verse 42 forms a contrast to verse 41; the announcement of a reward for kindness to the " little ones " (the disciples) is followed by a terrifying threat to all who cause one of these little ones to sin by putting a stumbling block in his way. The sequence is therefore justified by the subject matter. But the triad of parts of the body which can create occasions of sin is only superficially relevant. In giving scandal which causes a disciple of Jesus to sin, another person's faith is shaken and their salvation endangered; the guilty therefore incur the severest punishment at God's judgment—hence the drastic image of being sunk into the sea. The occasions of sin prompted by members of the body refer to moral temptations which originate within a man, which he himself must overcome at the root, by " cutting off " these members so as not to incur damnation.

The Greek word which has come into English as " scandal " has none of the sensational overtones it has for us. It is not a question of creating a stir, attracting publicity, but of an inner jeopardizing of the person to whom scandal is given. The origin of the word is not perfectly clear, but seems to suggest a fall or stumble caused by an obstacle or by a trap. The great mill-stone (literally " donkey millstone "), was a particularly large stone which in a fixed mill (as compared with a hand mill) rested on another stone and had a hole through the middle. It was called a donkey mill, either because a donkey was needed to turn it or because of the shape of the understone. It would be better, Jesus says, for anyone who deludes another person about the faith, to have a stone of that kind tied round his neck and be thrown into the sea. A forceful metaphor—typical of Jesus' command of language—which means that it would be better to be dead and destroyed than to rob another of his faith.

The group of sayings about parts of the body which occasion moral lapses exhibits the radical character of Jesus' moral demands. He seriously meant that people must do everything to gain a share in the kingdom of God (cf. Lk. 13:24). When the ultimate goal is in question, there can be no half-measures. In the present passage Jesus names " life " as the goal of man's personal existence which brings him true salvation, and then, with the same meaning, " the kingodm of God." It is well to be clear about this figurative language of the Bible, so as to avoid any false conclusions in regard to " eternal damnation." The imagery which later copyists inserted in the first and second sayings (vv. 44 and 46, omitted above), are intended to express the divine judgment of reprobation. Not " to enter into life," not to share in God's eternal life and his future kingdom, means to miss the transcendent goal set for man, and that is the most terrible lot that can befall a human being. His earthly life has been meaningless, and with his bodily death he succumbs forever to meaninglessness, to " eternal death," the destruction of his humanity designed for eternal life.

SAYINGS ABOUT SALT (9:49–50)

⁴⁹" *For everyone will be salted with fire.* ⁵⁰*Salt is good; but if the salt has lost its saltness, how will you season it? Have salt in yourselves, and be at peace with one another."*

Once again a group of sayings is added with a catchword, this time the word " fire." In the next, enigmatically brief but on closer reflection extremely incisive saying, the term is used in a different sense from that on hell. Probably a sacrificial rite is in mind. According to Mosaic law, every sacrificial gift had to be salted; the salt symbolized the covenant with God (Lev. 2:13). In the food offering, the wheat flour mixed with oil had incense added and was then committed to the fire (Lev. 2:14–16). Similarly in the sin offerings, the animals were sprinkled with salt before they were burnt (Ezek. 43:24). In the present saying the allusion to these sacrificial rites is only faint and symbolic; it is not what is salted that is put into the fire, the fire itself becomes the " salt." Fire and salt have become symbolic terms. The exact sense of " fire " cannot be determined. Usually the divine judgment is characterized by these terms, though, according to Luke 12:49, Jesus has come to " cast [bring] fire upon the earth," which appears to refer to the eschatological separation (cf. v. 51). The disciple is called upon to follow Jesus with his cross (Mk. 8 : 34), to lose his life for Jesus' sake (8 : 35), to allow himself to be consumed like a sacrificial offering. Only in this way will he show himself to be " salt," as one who has the power of discipleship within him. He will not be spared the test of the severest sufferings and of persecutions even to death. This seems to be the meaning of this figurative saying, at least for Mark.

The next saying about salt has a parallel in the tradition of Luke and Matthew, but in a different, extended form: tasteless salt is thrown away. The Mark version obviously means salt that is used for seasoning; when it loses its taste, its " saltness," there is no way of restoring it. Matthew connected the saying about salt with one about light, and addressed this unified saying —" You are the salt of the earth . . . the light of the world "— directly to the community of the disciples (5 : 13–16).

In the final saying, salt is conceived as something actually within the disciples as a power inhering in them. Perhaps the precept: " Have salt in yourselves " is intended as the lesson to be drawn. We must not be misled by the accompanying exhortation: " Be at peace with one another "; this was probably added by the evangelist in order to round off the group of sayings and link up with the beginning, the disciples' quarrel. If the disciples take to heart all that has just been said to them, they will inevitably overcome their quarrelsomeness. And even more is at stake—the imitation of Jesus, which demands a disciple's whole strength, his constancy in the world, the existence of the Church in the midst of unsympathetic and often hostile surroundings. Can there still be jealousy and quarrelsomeness among them? A serious consideration in every age in which Christ's Church has to hold its ground and perform its functions in an unbelieving environment. Only utter dedication to the service of Christ, and fraternal harmony strengthen them on their way in imitation of Christ.

Important Themes of Concern to the Church, and the Third Prediction of the Passion (10:1-45)

After the discourse to the disciples which is at the same time a word of warning to the later community, a new section is clearly indicated. The journey to Jerusalem continues, the region of Judea and east of the Jordan is reached (10:1); but the literary forms, too, change. The next following paragraphs are broader compositions and deal with important questions in the life of the Church: the indissolubility of marriage, the value set on children, the attitude to property and wealth. Then follows the third prophecy of the Passion, linked with a lesson to the disciples against ambition, and establishing a hierarchy of service for their society.

INDISSOLUBILITY OF MARRIAGE AND PROHIBITION OF DIVORCE (10:1-12)

[1]*And he left there and went to the region of Judea and beyond the Jordan, and crowds gathered to him again; and again, as his custom was, he taught them.* [2]*And Pharisees came up and in order to test him asked, " Is it lawful for a man to divorce his wife?"* [3]*He answered them, " What did Moses command you? "* [4]*They said, " Moses allowed a man to write a certificate of divorce, and to put her away."* [5]*But Jesus said to them, " For your hardness of heart he wrote you this commandment.* [6]*But from the beginning of creation, ' God made them male and female.'* [7]*For this reason a man shall leave his father and mother and be joined to his wife,* [8]*and the two shall become one.' So they are no longer two but one.* [9]*What therefore God has joined together, let not man put asunder."* [10]*And in the house the disciples asked him again about this matter.* [11]*And he said to them,*

" *Whoever divorces his wife and marries another, commits adultery against her;* [12]*and if she divorces her husband and marries another, she commits adultery.*"

The evangelist's geographical indication is vague and is intended more as theological emphasis—Jesus is coming to Judea, that is, he is already approaching Jerusalem. " Beyond the Jordan " may indicate the route taken; he would have reached Jericho by the nearby fords. Perhaps behind it there is an old piece of information which Mark fitted in afterwards. His theological intention, however, is evident in the statement that crowds gathered round him, and that, as his custom was, he taught them. The fact that Jesus is teaching emphasizes the significance of what he says in what follows. Similarly, it is pointless to ask where the Pharisees come from who unexpectedly approach, or why they raised this particular question during a journey. They are the opponents who lend weight to his decision.

The question itself is also a remarkable one, for Mosaic law gives a clear answer to it. Every married Jew could dismiss his wife by issuing a bill of divorce; all that was disputed was the grounds that made it possible. The explanation added by the evangelist that they came " to test him " is intended to show their cunning. The whole introduction is designed from the point of view of the Church, which had the greatest interest in this question and, as a result of Jesus' ruling, departed from Jewish (and pagan) practice. Jesus' reply is also remarkable in that he speaks each time of Moses' *command*, while his partners in debate speak of the *permission* (Mt. 19 is different). Mark is closer to the original intention of the Old Testament regulation, which gave some measure of protection to the divorced wife, because the certificate preserved her honor and freedom of action. Consequently the expression " for your hardness of heart " cannot be meant as a concession to the Jews' weakness, but as incriminating testimony against them, because they were incapable of fulfilling God's original intention. Only the Pharisees regard it as a mark of God's favor.

Jesus goes back to the Genesis account which he takes as expressing God's declared will before the giving of the Mosaic law. He infers from the two scriptural texts, Genesis 1:27 and 2:24, that God's intention in creating man and woman was that the married couple should form an indissoluble union. They have left their earlier family communities, which in the circumstances of those times enclosed people much more strongly than they do today and gave them security, they have come together to form a union, and now belong together inseparably. The line of thought follows the text of scripture: by the creation of the two sexes, God himself willed this union, and it is so close that from now on the two are one flesh (the emphasis is on " one," not on " flesh "). Jesus underlines this by the conclusion he draws: man and woman in marriage can only be regarded as a unity. God himself appears as the founder of marriage—some Jews thought this even in regard to marriages actually contracted —consequently man can no longer annul this union.

Jesus' Attitude to Children (10:13–16)

[13]*And they were bringing children to him, that he might touch them; and the disciples rebuked them.* [14]*But when Jesus saw it he was indignant, and said to them, " Let the children come to me, do not hinder them; for to such belongs the kingdom of God.* [15]*Truly, I say to you, whoever does not receive the kingdom of God like a child shall not enter it." * [16]*And he took them in his arms and blessed them, laying his hands upon them.*

Once again, there is no point in asking about the situation. Little children, such as are obviously involved here, would hardly have been taken on the pilgrimage to Jerusalem. The incident must have taken place at a halt on the journey, but no indication is given where this was. The disciples whom Jesus wanted to protect from too great a crowd (or perhaps they were scandalized at the desire to touch Jesus for " magical " purposes, cf. 5:27–31), are only introduced in order to give greater emphasis to Jesus' words and attitude. It is not an idyllic scene intended to show Jesus' benevolence and special kindness to children, but a decision of principle important for the Church. The Church is shown how it is to treat children. Perhaps, also, it is to be decided whether or not children are to be baptized in infancy. The three sayings of Jesus about children which have been preserved leave no doubt about his own favorable attitude to children.

Jesus described the " childlike " attitude as a model for all who are seeking the kingdom of God. What did he mean by this? In the first place we must rid ourselves of the idea that it denotes the child's " innocence." Even pagan antiquity spoke less of this than might be thought, the idea was foreign to the Old Testament, and Judaism developed a number of differing opinions. On the one hand, the child is not yet obliged to obey the law (until the thirteenth year, but a boy ought to have some practice beforehand); on the other, from conception or birth the child already has the " evil inclination." Jesus is therefore certainly not alluding to the child's moral attitude. But a predominantly psychological interpretation hardly does justice to his meaning either. Matthew, of course, in the context of the disciples' dispute over precedence, when Jesus places a child in their midst, inserts by way of explanation, " Whoever humbles himself like this child, he is the greatest in the kingdom of heaven " (Mt. 18:4); but that is his own interpretation, guided by the saying, " Whoever exalts himself will be humbled and whoever

humbles himself will be exalted " (Mt. 23 : 12; cf. Lk. 14 : 11;
18 : 14), an independent saying which essentially refers to future
exaltation by God. A " humble " attitude on the part of the
child is questionable. What cannot be disputed, on the other
hand, is its smallness, insignificance (at least in the opinion of
antiquity), its immaturity in the sense of undeveloped mental
capacities. To accept Jesus' message about the kingdom of God, and
therefore God's proffered salvation, guilelessly, openly, and trust-
fully, in obedient faith—that is perhaps what Jesus meant when
he called on people to receive the kingdom of God " like a
child." Perhaps we may say, even more concretely, that the child
says to his father " Abba " with childlike candor and familiarity,
and that this is precisely what those who want to enter the
kingdom of God must learn to do. In that case, Jesus drew this
saying from his own immediate relation to God and calls for an
attitude of which he himself has given the example.

If that is so, Jesus' love for children is understandable. They
have something of the candor and spontaneity, the confidence
and trust, which are indispensable for our relationship with God
and for accepting Jesus' message.

JESUS' ATTITUDE TO PROPERTY; THE RICH MAN AND DISCIPLE-
SHIP (10:17–22)

[17]And as he was setting out on his journey, a man ran up and
knelt before him, and asked him, " Good Teacher, what must I
do to inherit eternal life? " [18]And Jesus said to him, " Why do
you call me good? No one is good but God alone. [19]You know
the commandments: ' Do not kill, Do not commit adultery,
Do not steal, Do not bear false witness, Do not defraud, Honor
your father and mother.' " [20]And he said to him, " Teacher, all

these I have observed from my youth." [21] *And Jesus looking upon him loved him, and said to him, " You lack one thing; go, sell what you have, and give to the poor, and you will have treasure in heaven; and come, follow me."* [22] *At that saying his countenance fell, and he went away sorrowful; for he had great possessions.*

It is evident in what follows that the evangelist has something to say to the Church on the attitude to be adopted to wealth and poverty. For this purpose he has combined traditional material to create a larger composition with three parts: 1) Jesus' meeting with the rich man (vv. 17–22); 2) his talk with the disciples about wealth as an obstacle to entering the kingdom of God (vv. 23–27); 3) Peter's question about the reward of renunciation, and Jesus' answer (vv. 28–31). The traditional material is heterogeneous, but connected by the theme of property and its renunciation. It is important to note that the idea of discipleship is behind Jesus' answer in the first and third sections. This carries further for the Church the theme of following the cross (8 : 34). Even its dealings with earthly possessions are to be determined by that summons, and become a test whether Jesus' radical demand is being met. By the example of the rich man, the Church learns how dangerous a power wealth is, even for serious, committed people, and Jesus' words to the disciples emphasize this. Finally, however, the example of Jesus' first disciples, who left everything for his sake, is an encouragement for the later Church to enter on the same path of poverty.

Let us take a close look at the scene. The effusive fulsomeness of the man Jesus meets on the way is in striking contrast to Jesus' own reserve and sobriety. The man hurries up obsequiously and addresses him as " good teacher." Jesus corrects him sharply; God alone is good. This statement is explained by the situation. Speculations whether Jesus too regarded himself as a sinner are out of place. Yet even Matthew hesitated about keep-

ing the question and answer in this form, and modifies it to:
" What good deed must I do? " whereupon Jesus answers,
"Why do you ask me about what is good? " But dogmatic
difficulties are unnecessary if we take the saying in its context.
Jesus rejects such flattery—still a powerful warning against any
personality cult. He answers the question, nevertheless, for the
man is an honest inquirer, like the scribe who asks Jesus about
the greatest commandment of the law (Mk. 12:28). Quite a
number of people in Judaism at that time were preoccupied with
the question of what they should best do to gain entrance to
eternal life, the " life of the world to come." The man's question
was similar in scope to that of the scribe. Jesus maintains his
reserve and quietly, almost prosaically, reminds him of the ten
commandments. The fact that he only lists commandments from
the " second table," dealing with relations with human beings,
is explained by the fact that the question concerned action, the
practical accomplishment of the divine will. Jesus is in harmony
here with Jewish endeavor. His omission of acts of worship of
God certainly recalls his demand that love of God be proved by
love of the neighbor (cf. 12:33f.). We may say that Jesus is
inviting the man to make an examination of conscience and has
already touched on the critical point for him. The man passes
this test, however, and is able to answer calmly that he has
observed all these from his youth.

Only at this point does Jesus give the questioner his full
attention, looks at him and is pleased with him (" loved him ").
Then he plunges his demand deep into the man's heart: " You
[still] lack one thing; go, sell what you have . . ." Anyone
called to be his disciple is taken over completely, seized at his
weak point, because God wants him whole and entire. It is the
same radical demand as in the saying about following the cross,
but it is applied concretely to this man in his own particular

situation. This insistence on a total and rapid decision, by which a man devotes himself to Jesus and binds himself through him to the service of God, re-echoes in quite a few sayings about discipleship (cf. Mk. 1:16–20; Lk. 9:57–62; 14:26), and forms part of the special character of the discipleship relation which Jesus founded. To that extent these are essentially individual cases, and each concerns individual human beings called specially by Jesus. The early Church, however, transferred discipleship of this kind, which in reality was only possible in Jesus' time and was bound up with his earthly presence, to the period after Easter, and discerned in Jesus' particular summons to individuals the abiding vocation of all believers. Not everyone has to give away all that he possesses, just as not everyone has to lay down his life for Jesus and the gospel; but all must hear Jesus' utterly urgent summons, which concerns each in a different way. If we are going to regard that as a " counsel," we must also be clear that it can become a commandment for the individual. " Counsel " as opposed to " commandment " only means that decisions such as complete renunciation of personal property can never be demanded of all the faithful.

In the present case the rich man refuses Jesus' demand, and goes away sorrowing because he has great possessions. Nothing is said about his losing salvation; the New Testament always avoids expressing any " verdicts of damnation." The evangelist's intention is to give the Church a warning example. In exculpation of that rich man we may recall that Judaism never lost the Old Testament view that wealth is a blessing from God, although at certain times in some circles, poverty, too, was regarded as a way to God and " the poor " as standing in a special relation to God (cf. the first of the beatitudes). But in the present context, the man who abandons Jesus is not excused; his gloom betrays his reluctance and his sadness is a sign that he cannot detach himself from his treasures.

WEALTH AS AN OBSTACLE TO ENTRANCE INTO THE KINGDOM OF GOD (10:23–27)

²³*And Jesus looked around and said to his disciples, " How hard it will be for those who have riches to enter the kingdom of God! " ²⁴And the disciples were amazed at his words. But Jesus said to them again, " Children, how hard it is to enter the kingdom of God! ²⁵It is easier for a camel to go through the eye of a needle than for a rich man to enter the kingdom of God." ²⁶And they were exceedingly astonished, and said to him, " Then who can be saved? " ²⁷Jesus looked at them and said, " With men it is impossible, but not with God; for all things are possible with God."*

The particular case is now explained for the benefit of the Church. As a stylistic device, Mark uses Jesus turning to the disciples; at 3:34, too, Jesus had looked around and uttered a saying of particular concern to the Church. The saying which Mark introduces in this way probably ran as follows in the tradition: " How hard it is for the rich to enter the kingdom of God. It is easier for a camel to go through the eye of a needle than for a rich man to enter the kingdom of God." The evangelist has extended this traditional saying into a dialogue with the disciples, and commented on it. The disciples' dismay emphasizes the gravity and shocking severity of the saying. This leads to a repetition (v. 24b), the only purpose of which is probably to drive home the saying. The reflection which follows: " Then who can be saved? " is perhaps a clarification by the evangelist (whose style and manner are perceptible) for the community, in which Jesus' hard saying had been the subject of discussions. But the answer to the anxious question about salvation, the reminder that all things are possible to God, is in harmony with the mind of Jesus and is confirmed by other sayings of his (cf. Mk. 11:23f.; Mt. 19:11).

DISCIPLESHIP IN POVERTY AND ITS REWARD (10:28–31)

28Peter began to say to him, " Lo, we have left everything and followed you." 29Jesus said," Truly, I say to you, there is no one who has left house or brothers or sisters or mother or father or children or lands, for my sake and for the gospel, 30who will not receive a hundredfold now in this time, houses and brothers and sisters and mothers and children and lands, with persecutions, and in the age to come eternal life. 31But many that are first will be last, and the last first."

Peter's declaration in the name of the disciples who have left everything for Jesus' sake, stands in effective contrast to the attitude of the rich man who refused. And so the theme of the dangers of wealth is followed by that of " apostolic " poverty. The disciples' spokesman does not ask for reward, at least in Mark (it is different in Matthew); it is Jesus' reply which creates this impression. The evangelist wants to lead up to this statement of Jesus, which the community had preserved as it had the saying about the rich. According to the (earlier) tradition of the saying's source, Jesus once promised his closest disciples, the twelve, a special reward, although it is impossible to determine the actual words used. The original saying was concerned with " sitting on thrones, judging the twelve tribes of Israel " (cf. Mt. 19:28; Lk. 22:30). The promise in Mark picks out from the start *everyone* who has left everything for the sake of Jesus or the gospel, and is therefore addressed to the whole Church or at least to those in it who have renounced earthly goods and family circle for Jesus' sake. Mark, too, received the saying from tradition, as is shown by some additions which are unmistakably due to him: the double turn of phrase " for my sake and for the gospel " (cf. 8:35); the restrictive proviso " with persecutions "; perhaps the repeated list in verse 30 which the other evangelists omit. On the other hand, the distinction between " now, in this time " and the " age to come " (which is lacking in Matthew) was probably introduced into Jesus' own saying even at a pre-Marcan stage. Mark speaks nowhere else of the present and coming eon, nor did Jesus use this vocabulary as far as we can tell. His promises always refer to the eschatological goal, the kingdom of God or eternal life. Originally, therefore, the hundred-fold reward meant eternal life itself, but even before Mark the community had given a further interpretation to Jesus' words and spoken of a provisional " reward " even in the present age. They saw it bestowed on the disciples of Christ who renounced home, family, and possessions but found a new family and home in the Church.

In the context of Mark's scene, in the general perspective of the cost of discipleship, the words addressed to Peter are not intended merely as consolation but as a new summons. The disciples of that time, for whom Peter is spokesman, become an example for the later disciples of Christ. Mark also weakens the earthly " reward " by the addition of " with persecutions." Even if the faithful find a certain compensation in the many " brothers and sisters, mothers and children," as well as in the material welfare which they come to know in the bosom of the Church, they are nevertheless to realize that this is still the time of per-secution, distress, cross-bearing. The real " reward " is still ahead, the eternal life which they may expect in the world to come. Only then will the great reversal take place. Many who played the chief role on earth will be insignificant, whereas others who were in the background will occupy places of honor.

But is the motive of a reward not unworthy, almost intolerable? Does it not encourage the attitude of undertaking earthly " sacrifices " and deprivations in order to acquire as great a heavenly reward as possible, " eternal happiness "? And does this not lead to flight from the world and to the congregations' shutting themselves off in ghettoes, a policy which nowadays we recognize to have been mistaken and harmful, a source of frequent failure to the Church, which as a result evaded its duties to the world in the sphere of social action and necessary protest against the oppression of some sections of society? It is impossible in fact to deny such dangers or that the Church has incurred much guilt in the course of history. Even Jesus' words are liable to be misunderstood. But if we consider his original intention, striving for reward is excluded. He uses the *metaphor* of a hundredfold recompense in order to encourage the renunciation of earthly possessions at the call of the gospel. He wants in fact to guide his disciples away from egotistical striving for money and property in order to give themselves entirely to God. They are to use earthly goods according to God's will, that is, for the poor and needy. They acquire no claim on God thereby, but may expect to receive back from him as a gift all they renounce.

There are dangers also in finding a home in the Church. Those who seek in the society of their brothers and sisters in the faith a real substitute for what they have renounced or lost, have not yet grasped what the call to follow the cross really means. Jesus left even his closest disciples to die alone and abandoned—for all humanity. The Church is not primarily a refuge for the lonely but the assembly of all who renounce their own wills for Jesus' sake and the service of others. It is not a quiet corner away from the world, but a point from which to set off towards the world. As such, it has to equip and strengthen the faithful, give them confidence that they have like-minded people at their side, going the same way, trying to fulfill the same mission in the world. A community which is suffering oppression and persecution needs this certainty and reassurance (cf. 1 Pet. 5:9). The early Church certainly did not misinterpret its Lord, therefore, if as well as the unparalleled demand Jesus imposes, his human kindness is also constantly apparent.

THE THIRD PREDICTION OF THE PASSION (10:32–34)

[32]*And they were on the road, going up to Jerusalem, and Jesus was walking ahead of them; and they were amazed, and those who followed were afraid. And taking the twelve again, he began to tell them what was to happen to him,* [33]*saying, " Behold, we are going up to Jerusalem; and the Son of man will be delivered to the chief priests and the scribes, and they will condemn him to death, and deliver him to the Gentiles;* [34]*and they will mock him, and spit upon him, and scourge him, and kill him; and after three days he will rise."*

At this point Mark very deliberately inserts Jesus' third and longest prophecy of the Passion. It lends a special character to the dialogue on poverty, and forms an appropriate transition to the pericope which follows on ruling and serving; it is, as it were, the general accompaniment to all the questions and dialogues of this section. The Church can only understand Jesus' pronouncements and demands if it is conscious of the road to death which its Lord has entered upon with full deliberation, fully aware of what awaits him. This new prediction of his Passion, which lists his shameful sufferings in detail, also makes it clear that Jesus is already close to the place of his death.

The statement that the journey to Jerusalem was continuing, coming after 10:1 and 10:7, forms to some extent a new start yet maintains the idea of a continuous journey. A new detail is that Jesus is walking ahead (i.e. of the disciples). The disciples are " amazed " at this, that is, as the Greek verb implies, are seized with stupefaction and horror (cf. 1:27; 10:24); there must be some special meaning in the fact that Jesus went ahead. It will have to be understood in the sense in which Luke says at the very beginning of the journey, " He set his face to go to Jerusalem " (9:51). With inflexible determination, Jesus goes up to the holy city, in the hills, although he knows that Jerusalem is where his destiny will be fulfilled in a terrible way. Then " those who followed " are mentioned (a few manuscripts omit them); they must be the other people who were accompanying him (cf. 10:1). The twelve are then expressly distinguished from them. These remarks setting the scene are not made at random. In the person of " those who followed," Mark's readers, all the members of the Church, are once again specially addressed. " They were afraid." It is hard to see why, in the actual historical situation. The evangelist has aimed it at the faithful who shrink from suffering and shame. It was with good reason that he had added " with persecutions " at 10:30. The disciples who are amazed to see Jesus resolutely going ahead of them throw into higher relief the picture of Christ; those who follow represent the situation and attitude of the Church. The whole forms a striking picture of the pilgrim people of God, following its Lord timidly and hesitantly, perhaps in terror, yet drawn onwards by this " pioneer and perfector of [our] faith " (Heb. 12:2).

Jesus reveals to the twelve, but only to them, the things that await him, because only they are to be initiated into the mystery of his Passion (cf. 8:31). In comparison with the earlier predictions, it is noteworthy that the various stages and sufferings are enumerated. This time it is not so much a lesson (8:31; 9:31) as a disclosure of what does actually take place and is related in detail in the Passion narrative (chapters 14–15). It is precisely in the knowledge of all this that Jesus fearlessly goes on ahead of his companions. The things that are going to happen are listed in the order in which they came about: the proceedings before the Sanhedrin, with the condemnation to death and the delivery into the hands of the " Gentiles," that is, to the Romans; then various shameful sufferings which Jesus will undergo, to be mocked, spat upon (which denotes uttermost contempt), scourged, and finally executed. The mockery as king of the Jews by the Roman soldiers, during which the spitting is expressly mentioned (15:16–20), is in fact listed in Jesus' prophecy before the scourging (15:15), but this is because for Mark the scourging is more closely linked with the crucifixion (cf. the mode of expression in 15:15). It might be thought remarkable that the mode of death itself, crucifixion, is not given as the most shameful of all (a death reserved for slaves and criminals), as at Matthew 20:19. But except in the Passion narrative, the early Church avoids this, probably because in its preaching, death and resurrection go together. The reference to the resurrection is not lacking here (or in the earlier predictions) and the adjunct " after three days " indicates the rapid transformation brought about by God. This time the evangelist does not note any reaction on the part of the disciples; it seems as if their resistance is less and no question (cf. 9:32) is possible in view of Jesus' clear prediction about himself. His determined will to accept the suffering and his clear foreknowledge are what are to be impressed on the readers.

The three meanings of the Greek word " delivering up "— to betray, to deliver up to judgment, to hand on as tradition (in a theological sense)—converge and are suited to encourage reflection on the interplay of the insidious malice and cruelty of men with God's incomprehensibly allowing things to take their course, behind which there stands his saving design. The dark mystery of the Passion becomes all the more impenetrable when to all the shame and suffering inflicted by men there is joined the idea of abandonment by God; yet the Son of man entered into that uttermost darkness (cf. 15:34).

A Request by the Sons of Zebedee; Rule and Service (10:35-45)

35And James and John, the sons of Zebedee, came forward to him, and said to him, " Teacher, we want you to do for us whatever we ask of you." 36And he said to them, " What do you want me to do for you? " 37And they said to him, " Grant us to sit, one at your right hand and one at your left, in your glory." 38But Jesus said to them, " You do not know what you are asking. Are you able to drink the cup that I drink, or to be baptized with the baptism with which I am baptized? " 39And they said to him, " We are able." And Jesus said to them, " The cup that I drink you will drink; and with the baptism with which I am baptized, you will be baptized; 40but to sit at my right hand or at my left is not mine to grant, but it is for those for whom it has been prepared." 41And when the ten heard it, they began to be indignant at James and John. 42And Jesus called them to him and said to them, " You know that those who are supposed to rule over the Gentiles lord it over them, and their great men exercise authority over them. 43But it shall not be so among you; but whoever would be great among you must be your servant, 44and whoever would be first among you must be slave of all. 45For the Son of man also came not to be served but to serve, and to give his life as a ransom for many."

The request of the sons of Zebedee reflects their hopes and probably those of most of the disciples; they are still earthly ones. A delightful feature is the sly way they contrive to express what they want. They would like Jesus first of all to give them a blank check, as it were, for their unexpressed wish, but Jesus obliges them to show their hand. Their desire to sit to right and left of Jesus "in his glory" can hardly mean anything except that they expect his messianic rule to come on earth. The early Church was of course to apply "in your glory" to Jesus' transcendent, eschatological kingdom (cf. 8:38). The request of these disciples who had been called early (1:19f.) and were specially favored by Jesus (cf. 5:37; 9:2), affords a glimpse of their messianic hopes during Jesus' lifetime. These were still rather crude, and probably shared the usual view of the Jews of that age that the Messiah (the son of David) would establish an earthly kingdom; we surmise that Peter had the same idea of the Messiah at Caesarea Philippi (8:29f.).

Jesus' answer reveals—less clearly than his words to Peter (8:33)—the all too human mentality of the two disciples. They have not understood that the way of suffering and death is indicated for them in imitation of Jesus, before they can be with him "in glory." He reminds them of his own way. He has to drink a cup and be baptized with a baptism. The meaning of these two metaphors is explained by the Old Testament, where there are a number of references to the cup of God's wrath which he gives to his faithless people Israel or to the proud nations of the world to drink. "Stand up, O Jerusalem, you who have drunk at the hand of the Lord the cup of his wrath, who have drunk to the dregs the bowl of staggering" (Is. 51:17). "Take from my hand this cup of the wine of wrath, and make all nations to whom I send you drink it" (Jer. 25:15). It is a cup of horror and desolation (Ezek. 23:33); all the wicked of the earth must drain it (Ps. 75:8). It is not therefore simply a "bitter cup of suffering" but a symbol of the wrath and judgment of God. When Jesus applies the metaphor to his own Passion (Mk. 14:36 par.), it may also be implied that he is taking God's judgment upon himself and wills to bear the extremity of pain for men's sake. Similarly, the image of baptism signifies direct distress, a plunge into the waves. "All thy waves and billows have gone over me " (Ps. 42:7; cf. 69:2f.). It may be called a baptism of death, even if the metaphors do not necessarily signify physical death.

How far the disciples were from the mind of Jesus, is shown by their self-confident answer: We are able. They are ready to undertake the severest trials and sufferings as the price of the expected rule with their Lord, and they trust to their own strength. They have not yet understood that one must allow oneself to be led by God and that human pride is useless when it comes to bearing the heaviest blows. Desire for domination and power is an obstacle to following Jesus' path. And so Jesus tells them plainly that they, like himself, will indeed experience that cup and baptism, yet will not have any claim to rulers' thrones for all that. This answer sounds like a prophecy of their future, and it has sometimes been inferred that Jesus is fore-telling a martyr's death for the two brothers. James did in fact die a martyr at an early date (Acts 12:1f.); there is no firm proof in John's case, but the present passage is nevertheless sometimes quoted to show that he was soon put to death as a martyr. The question is not without its importance for the problem of the authorship of the fourth gospel, but less important than used to be thought. What Mark wants to say to his community is something different: God decides the lot of those who make great plans for themselves, and it is the disciple's business to allow God to decide what shall become of him. The allocation of places of honor and power in the future kingdom of God, like everything in the future, is left to the sole disposition of God.

The culminating saying about Jesus' own service to the point of the sacrifice of his life, is remarkable in several respects. It speaks of the " Son of man," of Jesus' mission and his atoning death. Early Christology has concentrated and crystallized here, but in a way which does not distort Jesus' thoughts and attitude. Despite his authority, he was not a ruler but a servant among men and did not lord it over anyone, even in the circle of his disciples. The pupil of a rabbi who came to him to learn the precepts of the law and the rules of scriptural interpretation, and to gain practice in living according to the law, was also under an obligation to perform personal services to his teacher. Jesus made no such claim; furthermore, at the last gathering with his disciples, he made a point, we might say, of performing services at table which were not those of the master of the house (cf. Lk. 22:27; Jn. 13:13f.). It is not unlikely that he meant this to be a mark of his love to the end (cf. Jn. 13:1). The early Church was right in regarding Jesus' Passion and death, accepted in obedience to God, as a work of uttermost service to mankind. It may have explained Jesus' loving service, in the light of his words over the cup (Mk. 14:24), as a vicarious atoning death, but this did not misinterpret his intention.

The metaphor of ransom falls into correct perspective precisely as the conclusion and culmination of the saying about service. Jesus' death is his greatest action deliberately performed, by which he fulfilled his life of service for others. The early Church recalled this attitude of Jesus above all in the celebration of the Eucharist, when it heard that Jesus willed with his blood shed "for many" to seal the perfect and definitive covenant of God with mankind (cf. 14:24). But, as the present saying shows, it also understood the duty that this entails for the Church. Just as God has accepted the sacrifice of his Son, so all who enter this covenant of God must be ready to follow Jesus in similar service.

Jesus' Entry into Jerusalem and His Last Ministry in the Capital
(10:46—13:37)

With 10:46 Jesus reaches Jericho, near which the pilgrims of the eastern route crossed the Jordan and took the ancient road up to Jerusalem (cf. Lk. 10:30). The cure of blind Bartimaeus, an early story precisely located in Jericho, belongs in character to the new section devoted to Jesus' entry into Jerusalem and his final ministry in the capital. This section falls into three parts: (1) signs and messianically important actions of Jesus before and on arrival in Jerusalem (healing of blind Bartimaeus, entry and popular ovation, cleansing of the temple and cursing of the fig-tree); (2) discussions and controversies with various groups in the Jewish capital; (3) prediction of the destruction of Jerusalem, and great eschatological discourse.

Once again all this is very methodically composed by the evangelist. The events on Jesus' arrival in Jerusalem show the tense atmosphere in the ancient city of God. He himself manifests his messianic dignity by symbolic actions, while at the same time his enemies' determination to remove him increases. This situation is then brought into an even sharper focus by Jesus' controversy with the leading representatives of Judaism. Of course these debates have an additional purpose, namely that of giving the Church community information on important questions on which Jesus had expressed his mind. Then the curtain falls on Jesus' public ministry. Teaching is next given privately to the disciples about the fate of Jerusalem and the time to come, which is marked by the sign of the end; that is the age in which Mark's Church is living. It receives guidance for its behavior in the afflictions which it has to undergo, externally by persecutions and sufferings, and also inwardly by deceivers and various kinds of temptations. This is eschatological doctrine, given to the Church for its life in this present, still evil, world epoch, but the ultimate purpose is not information but exhortation and encouragement to adopt a right attitude.

*Jesus' Symbolic Messianic Ministry
on Arrival in Jerusalem (10 : 46—11 : 25)*

What is striking in these externally closely connected paragraphs is Jesus' repeated and deliberate symbolic action. In the mind of the evangelist this seems to begin even with the cure of the blind man of Jericho, where Jesus does not forbid the loud acclamation " Son of David," but restores sight to this man who believes and follows him with faith. In the preparations for the entry, Jesus possesses foreknowledge, gives his disciples clear instructions, chooses quite deliberately the colt of a donkey on which no one had yet ridden, and allows himself to be acccompanied by bands of people. The action of the crowd, especially the cries of homage, underlines the obvious messianic character of the scene. One the way to the temple he curses a fig tree that bears no fruit—at first sight a pointless action, for it was not the season for figs, but in reality a symbolic action in the manner of the prophets. Then he drives the traders from the forecourt of the temple; this, too, was a demonstration with deeper implications. Finally, by the already withered fig tree, he exhorts the disciples to unswerving faith, confident prayer, and fraternal forgiveness. Jesus and the people, the disciples and the opponents, come on the scene in turn, well characterized in their various roles, but the figure of Jesus dominates the whole. He acts with authority as never before, yet he is surrounded by the suspicion and hatred of his opponents and enveloped in the gloom of the impending events. He himself sees his Passion approaching yet strides bravely towards it; the disciples witness signs which they only understand later and hear sayings which disclose their full meaning only in the situation and afflictions of the Church.

The Cure of the Blind Man at Jericho (10:46–52)

⁴⁶And they came to Jericho; and as he was leaving Jericho with

his disciples and a great multitude, Bartimaeus, a blind beggar,
the son of Timaeus, was sitting by the roadside. [47]*And when he*
heard that it was Jesus of Nazareth, he began to cry out and say,
" Jesus, Son of David, have mercy on me! " [48]*And many rebuked*
him, telling him to be silent; but he cried out all the more,
" Son of David have mercy on me! " [49]*And Jesus stopped and*
said, " Call him." And they called the blind man, saying to him,
" Take heart; rise, he is calling you." [50]*And throwing off his*
mantle he sprang up and came to Jesus. [51]*And Jesus said to him,*
" What do you want me to do for you? " And the blind man
said to him, " Master, let me receive my sight." [52]*And Jesus said*
to him, " Go your way; your faith has made you well." And
immediately he received his sight and followed him on the way.

Cures of the blind played a part in early tradition (cf. 8:22–26).
The numerous diseases of the eyes in the East had little prospect
of cure in those days, and the lot of those afflicted by them was
harsh. There was nothing for most of them but to beg (cf. Jn.
9:8). There was also the mental distress of lifelong darkness.
Consequently the blind are particularly representative of human
distress and helplessness.

The story of blind Bartimaeus is certainly based on early
tradition. The name, an Aramaic patronymic (bar Timai), has
no symbolic meaning. Rabbuni as a mode of address (cf. Jn.
20:16) is an old Aramaic form. The location of the event in
Jericho raises no difficulties either. Jericho, the " city of palms "
north of the Dead Sea, one of the oldest settlements in Palestine,
figures in the gospels only in the special Lucan tradition about
the chief tax collector Zacchacus (Lk. 19:1–10) and is mentioned
in the story of the good Samaritan (Lk. 10:30). Mark relates
this cure—the only one in the second part of his book—not
because it happened on the last stage of Jesus' journey to
Jerusalem, nor even, probably, to demonstrate Jesus' unbroken

healing power and undiminished mercy. This cure is narrated in a different way from that of Beth-saida (8:22-26). We hear of the loud cries of the beggar by the roadside, and the twice repeated cry " Son of David " rings in our ears. Apart from the Son of David discussion at 12:35-37, this is the only time in Mark's gospel that this Jewish messianic title is used, and Jesus allows it. Many in the crowd rebuke the man, but Jesus sends for him. He praises his faith with the same words—" Your faith has made you well!"—that he had used for the simple faith of the woman with a haemorrhage (5:34). After the cure the man does not simply go away, but follows Jesus on the way.

If due attention is given to the emphasis placed by the evangelist on this or that aspect of the story, the meaning of the cure of the blind man in precisely this context becomes clear. The crowds, as the readers have long realized, accompany Jesus, it is true, but without real faith, blind to his mission. Blind Bartimaeus, on the other hand, firmly and unswervingly believes in him as the Son of David, the Messiah, however people may rebuke him. His faith is not yet purified, any more than that of the woman in the crowds who touched the hem of Jesus' garments; but he believed in Jesus' goodness and power in which God's help is at hand for him. Faith of that kind is superior to both the cleverness of the scribes (cf. 12:35-37) and the obtuseness of the crowd. The blind man has had his own ideas about the man of Nazareth (cf. 1:24), takes no offense at his origin (cf. 6:1-6), and addresses him with full confidence. A man with such trust can become a disciple of Jesus and later accept the Church's confession of faith in Christ—but no, he follows him immediately and perhaps he actually did belong later to the Church like Simon of Cyrene who helped Jesus to carry the cross (15:21). For the Christian reader he becomes the model of a fearless confessor of faith and of a disciple who follows Jesus on his way to death.

For Mark, however, Jesus' behavior, too, is significant : it is surprising that he does not refuse the messianic title of Son of David, which, moreover, was a politically dangerous one. But now that he has taken the road to death and the goal is approaching where the divine designs are to be fulfilled, the barriers can fall and the messianic secret can be disclosed. The misconception of a political liberator is nevertheless not to be prevented, and Jesus will be executed as one. However, this does not prevent, but fulfills, God's secret plan. Jesus' death at the hands of men makes him, according to God's will, the true bringer of salvation. Jesus is the Messiah, but in a different sense from what the Jews expected. Unmistakably a line leads from the cry of the blind man at Jericho to the acclamations of the people at the entry into Jerusalem: " Blessed is the kingdom of our father David that is coming!" (11 : 10). This kingdom is coming, but once again not in the way the crowd thinks—as the kingdom of God comprising all nations, the " many " for whom Jesus' blood is poured out (14 : 24; cf. 10 : 45). It is a kingdom of peace, as Jesus' royal yet peaceful entry into Jerusalem on the colt of an ass indicates to the percipient. Jesus does not silence Bartimaeus and the crowd at the entry into Jerusalem. He goes his way, dutiful and obedient solely to him who has sent him. The Church, however, is called to follow him, as Bartimaeus did once he was cured. The healing was only a sign of saving faith. Just as faith makes a blind man well, has " saved " him with Jesus' help, so, too, faith which leads men to join and follow Jesus on his way of death bestows true health, ultimate salvation.

Jesus' Entry into Jerusalem (11:1–11)

¹*And when they drew near to Jerusalem, to Bethphage and Bethany, at the Mount of Olives, he sent two of his disciples, ²and said to them, " Go into the village opposite you, and*

C

immediately as you enter it you will find a colt tied, on which no one has ever sat; untie and bring it. [3]*If anyone says to you ' Why are you doing this? ' say, ' The Lord has need of it and will send it back here immediately.' "* [4]*And they went away, and found the colt tied at the door out in the open street; and they untied it.* [5]*And those who stood there said to them, " What are you doing, untying the colt? "* [6]*And they told them what Jesus had said; and they let them go.* [7]*And they brought the colt to Jesus, and threw their garments on it; and he sat upon it.* [8]*And many spread their garments on the road, and others spread leafy branches which they had cut from the fields.* [9]*And those who went before and those who followed cried out, " Hosanna! Blessed is he who comes in the name of the Lord!* [10]*Blessed is the kingdom of our father David that is coming! Hosanna in the highest! "* [11]*And he entered Jerusalem, and went into the temple; and when he had looked around at everything, as it was already late, he went out to Bethany with the twelve.*

This paragraph is well known to us from Palm Sunday, but has deeper implications which familiarity tends to make us overlook. Theological considerations have so determined its composition that it is practically hopeless to ask what precisely happened, what it meant to the accompanying crowds, and what impression it made on the public. Attempts that have been made on its basis to accuse Jesus of a messianic political intention are beside the point; this event plays no part at all in Jesus' trial. Many groups of pilgrims crowded into the holy city for the feast of the Passover, and there was nothing violent or sensational about Jesus' entry in itself. Messianic excitement of the crowd with political overtones could at most be inferred from the acclamations. " Blessed is he who comes in the name of the Lord " is a saying from a psalm which could be applied to every visitor to the temple, a liturgical text, just as the Hosanna is. The evangelist presents the whole scene, not for its historical interest but for theological purposes.

It is at once apparent that Mark fits the entry into Jerusalem as an important link in a chain of Jesus' actions. The journey up to Jerusalem is now reaching its goal; the last stage before is Bethphage and Bethany on the Mount of Olives. (The mention of two places and in that order is remarkable, because Bethphage is closer to Jerusalem.) Jesus stops, sends two disciples ahead to see about the animal he is to ride. He therefore has planned this kind of entry, foresees, in fact, how the disciples will find the colt, gives instructions how they are to behave, and accepts the honors and acclamations. All this demands closer consideration, but first let us see the end of the story as Mark tells it. Jesus enters not only Jerusalem but also the temple, and looks around attentively. There is no doubt that this is intended to prepare the readers for what happens the next day, the cleansing of the temple. This, too, was planned in advance by Jesus; it is not done spontaneously on the spur of the moment. Jesus knows what his Father has determined, and the prophecy of scripture which he must fulfill. Consequently the animal he is to ride must imply a reference to the prophecy of Zechariah 9:9: " Rejoice greatly, O daughter of Zion! Shout aloud, O daughter of Jerusalem! Lo, your king comes to you, humbly and riding on an ass, on a colt the foal of an ass." Jesus is not a political liberator coming with horse and chariot, but enters Jerusalem as prince of peace on the royal mount of ancient times (cf. Gen. 49:11). This emphasizes Jesus' dignity; he receives an animal that has not yet been put to use for riding or transport and the disciples spread their garments on it. Thus, poor but dignified, and surrounded by the people, Jesus enters the city of God.

Disciples and people each contribute in their own way to enhance Jesus' dignity. As the procession moves off, three actions are mentioned and each has a symbolic meaning. The disciples lay garments on the animal as saddlecloth, as was customary with great dignitaries. Instead of carpets the people spread garments on the road in front of Jesus; this, too, is an eastern custom, but with little meaning on a road that stretched almost two miles to Jerusalem.

It is, however, the acclamations of those walking in front of and behind Jesus which express the meaning. " Hosanna " (Hebrew: *hoshiah-na* = " Save now! ") is a cry for help and salvation which was familiar to the crowd from Psalm 118:25. This psalm, a liturgical thanksgiving, belongs to the so-called Hallel psalms (113–118), which were sung on the great festivals. At the Passover they were sung while the lambs were slaughtered in the temple, while at domestic celebrations these joyful songs were sung praising God for his saving deeds in the history of Israel. The following verse was originally (Ps. 118:26) a blessing on the pilgrims entering the temple, probably sung by the priests; all who come to the house of God are to be blessed in Yahweh's name. In the present context, Jesus is meant in a special way; for Christian readers " he who comes in the name of the Lord " is God's envoy absolutely as such, the saviour. The expression recalls John the Baptist's question, " Are you he who is to come, or shall we look for another? " (Mt. 11:3). But as the expression is not known to have been used as a messianic title, this is a Christian interpretation. The Jewish crowd need not have intended the acclamation as a profession of faith in Jesus as Messiah.

Perhaps Mark wanted to indicate by means of the designation " David, our father " that such hopes were rife among the pilgrims arriving for the feast. The " coming " kingdom would then still be future, even though the evangelist, by the juxtaposition of the two acclamations, points to the present. For him and his Christian readers, Jesus' coming itself is the dawn of the kingdom of God, in a different sense of course from what the

Jews expected. The mention of David recalls the cry of blind
Bartimaeus at Jericho, " Son of David, have mercy on me! " It
is the dialectic of the Christian messianic faith that the Jewish
messianic hope is fulfilled in Jesus, though not in the way the
Jews of that time expected. That is what will have led to the
peculiarly restrained formulation.

Yet another hosanna rounds off almost liturgically the acclamations of the crowd. This time " in the highest " is added,
which directs the gaze to God who, according to the Jewish conception, reigns enthroned in the heights of heaven. Thus, in the
Psalms of Solomon we read: " Great is our God and glorious,
dwelling in the highest " (18:10f.). By this the honor is given
to God, for he alone brings the coming kingdom. The evangelist
does not want to dismiss the shouts of that crowd as mistaken
hope, any more than the cry of Bartimaeus was: the only really
negative reaction as he sees it, was that of the leaders in Jerusalem, who are contrasted with the people (cf. 11:18, 32; 12:12).
But these opponents of Jesus do not figure in this scene. Taken as
a whole, the acclamations are designed for the Christian community, made transparent in meaning at least for its understanding. Jesus brings the saving reign of God, but does so precisely as " he who comes in the name of the Lord," just as God
has ordained. It is to God (" in the highest ") that all petition,
prayer, and thanks must be addressed. In substance, therefore,
these acclamations could be taken over into the Church's liturgy.

In Mark, the cleansing of the temple does not follow immediately, as it does in Matthew and Luke, but this can scarcely
mean that for him the crowd has dispersed. His intention is
probably simply to contrast the colorful entry with the scene in
the temple, which for him, framed as it is by the cursing of the
fig tree, is marked by contradiction to official Judaism. The
return to Bethany is often regarded as a precautionary measure,
taken because Jesus could not feel safe within the walls of Jeru-

salem. There can be no doubt that tradition preserved an historical memory of Jesus' having stayed during the last days before the Passover in this place outside the area in which the Paschal lamb had to be eaten; the anointing at Bethany supports this (14:3–9). But fear of the Jews, whom Jesus bravely confronts the next day is, in Mark's view, certainly not Jesus' motive. By the change of place (cf. 11:12, 19, 27) he is, rather, giving stage directions designed to separate the various scenes and perhaps also to characterize Jerusalem as the site of the rejection of God's envoy.

THE CURSING OF THE FIG TREE (11:12–14)

12On the following day, when they came from Bethany, he was hungry. 13And seeing in the distance a fig tree in leaf, he went to see if he could find anything on it. When he came to it, he found nothing but leaves, for it was not the season for figs. 14And he said to it, " May no one ever eat fruit from you again." And his disciples heard it.

The incident of the fig tree has been described as one of the most remarkable and puzzling stories in Jesus' ministry. Senseless anger seems to grip Jesus, and it is surely unreasonable to curse a tree that has no fruits although they are not in season? But rationalistic views of this sort simply show that we have lost all feeling for symbolic action.

In view of the fact that Jesus is protesting and demonstrating against the profanation of the Jewish sanctuary and that the Jewish leaders thereupon seek to destroy him (v. 18), it must concern the judgment on unbelieving, " barren " Judaism. Most likely it is an allusion to a passage in Jeremiah, not far from the passage referred to at the cleansing of the temple by the phrase " den of robbers " (Jer. 7:11): " Behold my anger and my wrath will be poured out on this place, upon man and beast, upon the trees of the field and the fruit of the ground; it will burn and not be quenched " (7:20). God's wrath is already unleashed against obdurate Judaism, in particular against its leaders, the " chief priests and the scribes " (v. 18), who do not understand Jesus' action in the temple and shut their hearts in unbelief. In this case, Jesus' symbolic action is primarily an expression of the rejection of the unbelieving Jews, and only remotely a threat of the external judgment. Much worse is the inner withering, the atrophy of true faith, which despite all external piety, despite all splendid liturgy, makes it barren and reprehensible in God's eyes.

The Cleansing of the Temple (11:15–19)

[15]*And they came to Jerusalem. And he entered the temple and began to drive out those who sold and those who bought in the temple, and he overturned the tables of the money changers and the seats of those who sold pigeons;* [16]*and he would not allow anyone to carry anything through the temple.* [17]*And he taught, and said to them, " Is it not written, ' My house shall be called a house of prayer for all the nations '? But you have made it a den of robbers."* [18]*And the chief priests and the scribes heard it and sought a way to destroy him; for they feared him, because all the multitude was astonished at his teaching.* [19]*And when evening came they went out of the city.*

As with the entry into Jerusalem, it is scarcely possible now to reconstruct the precise historical circumstances of the cleansing of the temple, what exactly was done and what were the direct effects. It is pointless to speculate how Jesus could effectively do anything against the numerous money changers and sellers of sacrificial animals in the extensive temple area, probably in the Court of the Gentiles. There is no suggestion that he used his disciples and followers. We don't even hear of any resistance by those affected. As Mark presents it, it is once again a symbolic prophetic action. The temple authorities had permitted money changers and sellers of sacrificial victims to set up their stalls in the Court of the Gentiles, which was separated from the inner courts. The money changers were needed because the temple dues required annually from every Jew could only be paid in the old (Tyrian) temple money, half a shekel per person (cf. Ex. 30:13; about a dollar). For the temple authorities who issued the licence and for the money changers who levied a fee, it was also good business. Sacrificial animals, in particular doves, the prescribed offerings for poorer people (cf. Lk. 2:24), had to be available. One particular detail is noted only by Mark: Jesus would not allow anyone to carry anything through the temple.

Mark also quotes a text from Jeremiah and in addition precedes it, through the cursing of the fig tree, with an unmistakable threat. His intention is certainly not to weaken in any way Jesus' vehement criticism or blunt the edge of his demonstration against the Jewish temple authorities. Nevertheless, he links Jesus' protest with a prophecy about the eschatological temple which will stand open to all nations, that is, to the Gentiles as well.

But what has Mark in mind in deliberately quoting " My house shall be called a house of prayer for all the nations "? The answer lies in the saying about the temple at 14:58, " I will destroy this temple that is made with hands, and in three days I will build another, not made with hands." However obscure the saying in itself, particularly its first part, it is evident that, at least as Mark understands it, the temple not made by human hands is the Church. The important point for the Gentile Christian evangelist is that all nations, including the Gentiles, are admitted. Against the background of the judgment of condemnation on the Jewish people and the destruction of the magnificent temple of Jerusalem (13:1f.), the prophecy about the house of prayer for all the nations takes on a clear meaning. The new temple will be quite different, it will not be built with human hands at all, and must no longer be desecrated by unworthy traffic.

The stone temple itself had been built for quite a different purpose; it is men who have made it a " den of robbers." To understand this harsh expression, the prophecy must be read in its context (Jer. 7:1-15). It is quite wrong to try to read into the word used for " robbers," which in Greek can also mean " guerrillas, irregulars," an allusion to the Zealots. The harsh expression is deliberately chosen by the prophet to scourge the lawless immoral conduct of his Jewish contemporaries who, into the bargain, boasted of the temple and tried to cover up their evil deeds by the temple cult. "Amend your ways and your doings, and I will let you dwell in this place. Do not trust in these deceptive words: 'This is the temple of the Lord, the temple of the Lord, the temple of the Lord. . . . Has this house, which is called by my name, become a den of robbers in your eyes? Behold, I myself have seen it" (7:3f., 11). More is involved, then, than removing abuses or reforming the temple cult; what is in question is a new and different worship of God, moral conversion, the accomplishment of the will of God in personal and social life.

The expulsion of the buyers and sellers from the forecourt of the temple is a symbol that points to the future. The true temple will be the eschatological community, a " house of prayer " and a place of holiness, of the moral worship of God. That is how Mark understands it; John not only places the same scene at the beginning of Jesus' ministry but also interprets it differently—Christologically. The conception of the community as the temple of God is not an entirely new idea, for there are clear evidences of it in the Qumran literature. This Jewish sect regarded itself as

" a holy house for Israel and a circle of the all holiest for Aaron,"
" a House of Holiness for Israel, an Assembly of Supreme Holiness for Aaron " (1 QS 8:5f., 9). The Christian Church, on the other hand, is to be a house of prayer *for all nations*.

But Jesus' protest falls on deaf ears in the Judaism of that time among the " chief priests and scribes," and its only result is that they want to get rid of this awkward critic. The multitude is amazed at his teaching, frightened by what Jesus does and demands. But the Christian Church is to understand that Jesus' criticism, prophecy, and teaching constitutes a permanent warning. In the evening Jesus leaves the city, and, for Mark, this too perhaps is a sign that Jesus is turning away from the old holy city and abandoning to their own resources those who do not seek God with a sincere heart.

CONVERSATION WITH THE DISCIPLES BY THE WITHERED FIG TREE (11:20–25[26])

²⁰As they passed by in the morning, they saw the fig tree withered away to its roots. ²¹And Peter remembered and said to him, " Master, look! The fig tree which you cursed has withered." ²²And Jesus answered them, " Have faith in God. ²³Truly, I say to you, whoever says to this mountain, ' Be taken up and cast into the sea,' and does not doubt in his heart, but believes that what he says will come to pass, it will be done for him. ²⁴Therefore I tell you, whatever you ask in prayer, believe that you receive it, and you will. ²⁵And whenever you stand praying, forgive, if you have anything against anyone; so that your Father also who is in heaven may forgive you your trespasses." (²⁶" But if you do not forgive, neither will your Father who is in heaven forgive your trespasses.")

As often with Mark a conversation with the disciples interprets for the community the even deeper meaning of Jesus' teaching. His answer to Peter's remark that the fig tree has withered contains a lesson on prayer for the Church, which has to be a " house of prayer " (v. 17). The evangelist has skillfully fitted it into the situation when, next morning, Jesus and his disciples are passing the fig tree which has withered in the meantime. He uses this sign of Jesus' power as an object lesson for the Church about the power of faith. But the exhortation to confident faith becomes in verse 24 an exhortation to pray, and the instruction on prayer is carried farther than the requirement of faith (v. 25). This final saying in which the community is admonished to mutual forgiveness is confirmation that it is the Church which is in view and which is to be the new temple of God. These verses, which bring together originally independent sayings of Jesus, must therefore be read in close connection with the cleansing of the temple and Jesus' quotation from scripture.

The saying about the faith which moves mountains (and which in Matthew is even more closely adapted to the withered fig tree) is an old saying of the Lord which the early Church pondered a good deal. In another context and in a different form in each case, it is also attested in the sayings source at Matthew 17:20 and Luke 17:6. Common to this tradition is the phrase " faith as a grain of mustard seed," and according to the proverbial meaning of mustard seed as something small, minimal (cf. Mk. 4:31), it means that even a very slight amount of " faith " is capable of effecting unbelievable things.

But what is " faith " in this sense? An absolutely radical and unshakable trust in God, who is greater, wiser, and more powerful than man. That is in fact the original meaning of the Hebrew verb, which still echoes in the ancient prayer word " Amen." It means saying Amen to God, taking one's stand and building on the firm ground of God and his word. It is not a blind, irrational, and emotional expectation of what is humanly impossible, but faith in the God who is revealing himself, whose word and promises are trusted with unshakable confidence because he is God.

The present passage also concerns intercessory prayer of petition. Mark's purpose is clear, however, in this and the following saying, from the word previously used, which denotes prayer in a quite general sense. He wants the Church to realize it is a " house of prayer." Because it is God's eschatological community, it has God's promise of a hearing. But, of course, the community itself must believe this so certainly that it is convinced even as it prays that it has already received what has been asked.

The last saying deals with a condition which is also included in the " Our Father." When we pray to God and ask him for forgiveness of our sins, we must also forgive those people who have been guilty of some fault in our regard. This saying, too, is expressed in the plural and concerns common prayer. In the community of Jesus' disciples, there has to be true fraternal forgiveness. Without it, prayer to the Father is dishonest and ineffectual. This thought is so indissolubly attached to the petition of the Lord's prayer that it impressed itself deeply on the early Church, and the present saying clearly refers to it (" your Father who is in heaven," " your trespasses," the only occasion Mark uses this word).

Jesus' promise always includes a strict claim. However lofty the saying about the temple which stands open to all the nations, its realization places the greatest responsibility on the community to which it applies, and the withered fig tree remains a permanent reminder of this.

Controversy with Leading Circles in Jerusalem (11 : 27—12 : 44)

Jesus' days in Jerusalem are filled with controversies of several kinds. The section is introduced by the question of Jesus' authority, which is put to him by the Sanhedrin; the three groups which it comprised are expressly mentioned (11:27; cf. 8:31), which emphasizes the official character of the inquiry. In the course of further discussions, Jesus meets representatives of leading groups in Judaism of that time (Sadducees and Pharisees). He avoids an open answer to the question of his authority, but counterattacks with the parable of the wicked husbandmen. The concluding quotation from scripture (12:10f.) makes plain the situation in the history of salvation: Jesus is the stone rejected by the builders which God has made into the cornerstone. This fulfills Jesus' prophecy at 8:31: in God's plan the Son of man has to be rejected by the elders, the chief priests and the scribes. A delicate theological touch is that the official representatives of Judaism reject Jesus, whereas a simple woman of the people receives high praise and becomes the representative of those who fulfill the will of God by what they do.

THE QUESTION OF AUTHORITY (11:27–33)

27And they came again to Jerusalem. And as he was walking in the temple, the chief priests and the scribes and the elders came to him, 28and they said to him, " By what authority are you doing these things, or who gave you this authority to do them? " 29Jesus said to them, " I will ask you a question; answer me, and I will tell you by what authority I do these things. 30Was the baptism of John from heaven or from men? Answer me." 31And they argued with one another, " If we say, ' From heaven,' he will say, ' Why then did you not believe him? ' 32But shall we say, ' From men '? "—they were afraid of the people, for all held that John was a real prophet. 33So they answered Jesus, " We do not know." And Jesus said to them, " Neither will I tell you by what authority I do these things."

The demand of the Sanhedrin for an explanation refers to the cleansing of the temple; only the evangelist's arrangement of his material has postponed it. The interrogation sounds objective and cool. The two parties envisage the two possibilities: Does Jesus claim authority of his own to act in this way, and, if so, what kind of authority is it? Or is he appealing to a delegated authority received from another? Jesus is to be forced to state plainly who he considers himself to be. We may suppose that the members of the Sanhedrin would then have looked for some charge to bring against Jesus, for example that he was a false prophet or a "seducer" of the people. But it does not come to that, because Jesus puts a counter-question to them and forces them to disclose their own attitude of mind. He asks them whether John's baptism was from God (" from heaven ") or from men, that is to say, whether they regarded John the Baptist as a true or false prophet. This question embarrassed them considerably: the evangelist expresses this vividly by the arguments they exchange among themselves or turn over in their minds. (In 2:6 he says more explicitly of the scribes "in their hearts," and in 8:16 of the disciples, "with one another.") If they admit that John's baptism was from God, Jesus can convict them of unbelief; at the same time they do not dare to contest it, because the people regard John as a true prophet sent by God. The formulation is rather clumsy but expresses very well the fact that their arguments do not flow from the point at issue itself but only concern their personal position and prestige—a severe but just criticism of men who, despite outward appearances, were not concerned about the cause of God but only about themselves. Their answer, "We do not know," is an evasion, which discredits them as leaders of the people and, what is worse, betrays their religious vacuity. Unbelief unmasks itself, even if it twists and turns and is skillful with words. Because of their answer, Jesus refuses to give the information they seek, and they have to admit defeat. That is so clear that the evangelist does not expressly say so; Jesus' refusal is the conclusion, an ominous final note.

Much can also be learned from Jesus' answer regarding discussion and debate between faith and unbelief. There are no rigorous proofs for people who do not want to believe. In theological argument with Judaism the early Church appealed in support of its belief in Jesus Christ to the testimony of the great preacher and baptist John, as all the gospels show. But it was also aware that the link between John and Jesus, the mutual respect and recognition of these two men who came forward in the name of God, John's reference to the greater who was to come after him, were not sufficient to win recognition of Jesus' divine mission and messiahship. Those who will not be convinced by the whole picture presented by Jesus in his words and actions while on earth, that God speaks and acts through him, cannot be set right by argument. Faith has good grounds in its favor, but unbelief finds counterarguments in its own support. But unbelievers should not think they can claim reason and logic exclusively for themselves. As soon as they are forced to show their hand, they betray their own assumptions which in fact presuppose unbelief.

THE PARABLE OF THE WICKED HUSBANDMEN (12:1–12)

[1]*And he began to speak to them in parables. "A man planted a vineyard, and set a hedge around it, and dug a pit for the wine press, and built a tower, and let it out to tenants, and went into another country.* [2]*When the time came, he sent a servant to the tenants, to get from them some of the fruit of the vineyard.* [3]*And they took him and beat him, and sent him away empty-handed.* [4]*Again he sent to them another servant, and they wounded him in the head, and treated him shamefully.* [5]*And he*

sent another, and him they killed; and so with many others, some they beat and some they killed. ⁶*He had still one other, a beloved son; finally he sent him to them, saying, ' They will respect my son.' * ⁷*But those tenants said to one another, ' This is the heir; come, let us kill him, and the inheritance will be ours.' * ⁸*And they took him and killed him, and cast him out of the vineyard.* ⁹*What will the owner of the vineyard do? He will come and destroy the tenants, and give the vineyard to others.* ¹⁰*Have you not read this scripture: ' The very stone which the builders rejected has become the head of the corner;* ¹¹*this was the Lord's doing, and it is marvelous in our eyes'? " * ¹²*And they tried to arrest him, but feared the multitude, for they perceived that he had told the parable against them; so they left him and went away.*

Jesus' real answer to the Sanhedrin is the parable of the wicked husbandmen, for in the editorial link (12:1) it is expressly said that Jesus began to speak in parables " to them," that is, to the same persons he had been addressing in 11:27-33. Only one parable follows, so the expression " to speak in parables " emphasizes the use of the parable as such, which is intended to convey something in a vivid and concrete way, yet produces a different effect on the hearers (cf. 4:10f.). According to the concluding statement, the members of the Sanhedrin realized that he had told the parable against them (v. 12); in fact, the parable is so transparent that any misunderstanding seems quite impossible. Consequently the point of the " speaking in parables " cannot be that it is unintelligible (cf. also 4:33); nevertheless there is something obscure about it, in a very much deeper sense; in unreceptive, unbelieving people it produces a lack of perceptiveness (4:12) or hardening of the heart (cf. 8:17). That is the terrible thing—although the parable is rationally intelligible, it does not lead to true insight, reflection, and change of heart, but hardens those people in their attitude of ill will: those it concerns are not really concerned. The Jewish leaders, before whose eyes a mirror of their own behavior is held up, hear the warning (v. 9), but do not listen to it. They confirm the role attributed to them and would willingly have arrested Jesus then and there but were afraid of the multitude (v. 12). It is Mark's view, already perceptible in the fourth chapter, that Jesus' speaking in parables exercises a critical, discerning function, directly productive of either salvation or calamity.

If the Christian community was already familiar with a parable of Jesus of the kind described, its present form is convincingly explained. The vineyard, which Jesus himself had most probably already chosen with a view to Israel, was described in terms of the Greek text of Isaiah 5:1f.; the servants were thought of as the prophets; the son was called the only son and "beloved" in accordance with the heavenly voice of 1:11 and 9:7; the Gentiles were thought of as the "others" to whom the vineyard is given. Above all, the significance of its Lord was brought out by means of the appended scriptural quotation about the cornerstone. The scriptural quotations in fact make it possible to establish even more precisely that this was done by Hellenistic Jews converted to Christianity. Mark could take over this Christian allegorical version for his hearers. Matthew carried the allegorization even further, for with him the owner of the vineyard twice sends out several servants who are ill-treated, killed, or stoned exactly as described in the lament over Jerusalem which follows: "O Jerusalem, Jerusalem, killing the prophets and stoning those who are sent to you! How often would I have gathered your children together . . ." (23:37). He (and Luke) also describe the son's killing as done outside the vineyard, perhaps because Jesus was crucified outside the gates of Jerusalem (cf. Heb. 13:12f.). By a glance of this kind into the theological workshop of the early Church and the evangelists, we

learn with them to understand the mysterious events as con-
forming to God's plan prepared beforehand in sacred history.

THE QUESTION OF TRIBUTE TO CAESAR (12:13–17)

¹³*And they sent to him some of the Pharisees and some of the
Herodians, to entrap him in his talk.* ¹⁴*And they came and said
to him, " Teacher, we know that you are true, and care for no
man; for you do not regard the position of men, but truly teach
the way of God. Is it lawful to pay taxes to Caesar, or not?*
¹⁵*Should we pay them, or should we not? " But knowing their
hypocrisy, he said to them, " Why put me to the test? Bring me
a coin, and let me look at it." ¹⁶And they brought one. And he
said to them, " Whose likeness and inscription is this? " They
said to him, " Caesar's." ¹⁷Jesus said to them, " Render to Caesar
the things that are Caesar's, and to God the things that are
God's." And they were amazed at him.*

The purpose of this famous scene of the coin of the tribute is
not to record a politically explosive situation, extremely dangerous
for Jesus, from which he extricated himself with great skill.
Certainly it is intended to show his superiority over his double-
tongued, cunning enemies, who seek to " entray " him (the word
tongued, cunning enemies, who seek to "entrap" him (the word
point of this pericope from the tradition is not the historical
situation, which is rather vague, but Jesus' answer, which provide sa guideline for the Church. The evangelist will certainly
have drawn on a collection of four disputes (12: 13–37) on very
different but in each case important themes. It was customary
among the Jews to submit problems of this sort to a rabbi for
decision. They were classified as questions on points of law,
questions intended to ridicule some tenet, questions on funda-

mental principles of a good life, and questions dealing with an apparent conflict between two texts of scripture. The four pericopes of 12:13–37 may correspond to this schema. At all events, Jesus is very definitely presented as a teacher who provides masterly solutions to difficult problems and whose answers are unsurpassable and permanently valid.

Two questions are involved, but the essential principle is raised first. Is it legitimate to pay the poll tax to the emperor, thereby acknowledging his rule over Israel? The general view in antiquity was that payment of tribute and taxes was equivalent to submission to the established régime. The poll tax to the Roman emperor was small in itself (1 denarius = about 30 cents), but it involved a matter of principle, and was therefore extremely hateful to the Jews. Next, the Pharisees ask about the concrete course of action to be taken. Are they actually to pay the tax, though at heart rejecting it? They want to compel Jesus to give an unequivocal answer. Jesus sees through their trickery and forces them to show their hand, just as he had done over the question of authority. That is the sole purpose of what he does. They themselves must bring him a silver tribute coin and thereby admit that they use the imperial money. They themselves must state that the coin bears the likeness and inscription of the emperor. Coins of the ruling emperor, Tiberius, are extant; the inscription runs: Tiberius, emperor, son of the divine Augustus. By doing so, they have unmasked themselves —they submit to the Roman rule. If they are to get him to give a different answer, it will have to be by cunning.

But Jesus himself does not avoid a decision. The emperor must receive what he has a claim to; the Greek word translated as " render " underlines that it is his right. The debt due to him should be discharged by paying the tax, and as the quite general formulation shows, duties to the State generally are to be fulfilled. Jesus, however, is not content with this answer, but adds on his own initiative, " And [render] to God the things that are God's." All the emphasis is here. The duties to God are much more important. Jesus goes beyond the question put to him and directs attention to what for him is most important—to give God what is his, to place oneself entirely at his disposal. The State with its order and its rights is not ultimate. God has a prior and higher claim on man.

The meaning of this pronouncement is not easy to grasp and its interpretation is disputed. Certainly Jesus is not intending to set up two separate orders, one earthly and human, the other a divine order remote from earthly things. God has claims on man even in the social and political domain. But this latter is not to be made an absolute; it has only limited validity. Even in the Jewish attitude to the pagan State, reserves were apparent. The state authority must not affect God's honor, suppress his commandments, forbid his worship, must not divinize itself and set itself in the place of God; it has to serve justice and human welfare and take responsibility for the way it exercises its power. But Jesus went even farther than this and positively expressed God's pre-eminence, and thereby indicated that the State is only a dependent and provisional reality. For Jesus, the earthly authorities occupy the historical place appointed by God, and history is advancing towards an ultimate which God will bring about, his eschatological kingdom of peace and salvation. Hence this saying of Jesus will bear the same meaning as his precept, " Seek first [God's] kingdom! " (Mt. 6:33). Jesus rejects political radicalism and revolution (represented in those times by the Zealots), just as he restrains pure interiority and flight from the world. His pronouncement is made so fundamental and far-reaching that it retains its validity in the most diverse historical circumstances and situations, although it requires appropriate application and new decisions in each.

THE QUESTION OF THE RESURRECTION OF THE DEAD (12:18–27)

[18]*And Sadducees came to him, who say that there is no resurrection; and they asked him a question, saying,* [19]"*Teacher, Moses wrote for us that if a man's brother dies and leaves a wife, but leaves no child, the man must take the wife, and raise up children for his brother.* [20]*There were seven brothers; the first took a wife, and when he died left no children;* [21]*and the second took her, and died, leaving no children; and the third likewise;* [22]*and the seven left no children. Last of all the woman also died.* [23]*In the resurrection whose wife will she be? For the seven had her as wife."* [24]*Jesus said to them, " Is not this why you are wrong, that you know neither the scriptures nor the power of God?* [25]*For when they rise from the dead, they neither marry nor are given in marriage, but are like angels in heaven.* [26]*And as for the dead being raised, have you not read in the book of Moses, in the passage about the bush, how God said to him, ' I am the God of Abraham, and the God of Isaac, and the God of Jacob '?* [27]*He is not God of the dead, but of the living; you are quite wrong."*

The Sadducees who come on the scene and engage in debate, rejected the belief in a resurrection of the dead which widely prevailed in Judaism at that time. The question of the resurrection of the dead is propounded in terms of an extreme case. According to a stylistic device customary among rabbis, it is an ironical question, not intended to ridicule the belief but to exhibit its difficulties and present a *reductio ad absurdum*. The assumption behind the argument is the so-called levirate marriage prescribed in Deuteronomy 25:5ff. The brother-in-law (*levir*), the unmarried brother of a man who died without male issue, was under an obligation to marry his sister-in-law, and his sons counted as sons of the dead man. The rule was based on the social and economic conditions of earlier times and ensured the succession to landed property, but even in Old Testament times it had been repressed.

Jesus answers the Sadducees' irony very seriously. They do not really know scripture, do not penetrate its profounder meanings. Nor do they know the power of God which is capable of acting in ways other than those that human reason comprehends. Thus, in the world to come, God disposes things differently from what they are now in this world. The idea of the new creation, which was familiar to Judaism, is taken up by Jesus and carried to its conclusion. He says that after the resurrection, sexual and conjugal relationships will no longer exist. They (men) do not marry, nor are they (women) given in marriage. This means that the corporal life of the risen will be quite different from life on earth. Jesus illustrates this important idea by the remark that they " are like angels in heaven." Here, too, Jesus is following Jewish tradition. According to the *Book of Enoch,* the angels have no wives, " for the spirits of heaven have their dwelling in heaven " (15 : 7).

Jesus firmly maintains the fact of the resurrection of the dead (or, " from the dead," i.e. from the world of the dead), and supports it by a special scriptural proof. He refers to the famous passage in which God appears to Moses in the bush which is burning yet not consumed, and reveals his name to him (Ex. 3 : 1-6, 13-15). God says " I am the God of your father, the God of Abraham, the God of Isaac, and the God of Jacob." Jesus' argument has often been understood to be that God is a God of the living, therefore those patriarchs must still be alive and one day will attain full life, that is, resurrection. But this certainly does not represent Jesus' thought. For the Jews, God's affirmation that he is the God of the fathers reveals his constancy and fidelity, his faithfulness to the covenant which he had made with the patriarchs and the promises which he had given them. These referred to a numerous progeny and the continued existence of the nation (cf. Gen. 17:7). Now for an Israelite, bodily existence was necessary to a full and complete life; consequently God's promise cannot be fulfilled in a life which ends with bodily death. Jesus infers the eschatological resurrection of the dead from God's fidelity to the covenant.

If we were once again to insist on imagining the resurrection in a crudely material way as a resurrection of corpses, as a coming to life again on this earth, as a new beginning of the life that was interrupted by death, we should in fact be falling back into the outlook of Jewish apocalyptic. Belief in the future and for us unimaginable resurrection of the dead stands and falls with belief in the transcendence of human personal existence which is to be fulfilled in God (cf. commentary on Mk. 8:35ff.). And if we take this belief seriously, the inclusion of the whole man, with his corporeality, in the life of perfect fulfillment with God, is perfectly logical and meaningful. For only if God takes us with our whole humanity and makes us share in his life is the transcendence which faith affirms no longer another and alien world, but the perfect accomplishment of our world, an accomplishment which we hope for from God's power, goodness, and fidelity, as the ultimate goal of our human life.

THE QUESTION OF THE GREATEST COMMANDMENT (12:28-34)

[28]*And one of the scribes came up and heard them disputing with one another, and seeing that he answered them well, asked him, "Which commandment is the first of all?"* [29]*Jesus answered, "The first is, 'Hear, O Israel: The Lord our God, the Lord is one;* [30]*and you shall love the Lord your God with all your heart, and with all your soul, and with all your mind, and with all your strength.'* [31]*The second is this, 'You shall love your neighbor as*

yourself.' There is no other commandment greater than these."
[32]*And the scribe said to him, " You are right, Teacher; you have
truly said that he is one, and there is no other but he;* [33]*and to
love him with all the heart, and with all the understanding, and
with all the strength, and to love one's neighbor as oneself, is
much more than all whole burnt offerings and sacrifices."* [34]*And
when Jesus saw that he answered wisely, he said to him, " You
are not far from the kingdom of God." And after that no one
dared to ask him any question.*

Once again Mark contrives to link the preceding pericope with
the new discussion. A scribe, in view of the circumstances probably a Pharisee, has been listening to Jesus' controversy with the
Sadducees. He has been surprised at Jesus' clear answer and
agrees with him. So he puts a new question to Jesus, once
again of a quite different kind, regarding the accomplishment
of the divine law, the best possible way of carrying it out in daily
life. There is no question this time of putting Jesus to the test
or of trapping him in his speech. It is a learned or doctrinal
debate. Jesus' answer, which the scribe in Mark accepts approv-
ingly and develops, was of the very greatest importance for the
early Church. The commandment of love is the core of Christian
ethics and is repeatedly recalled in early Christian paraclesis
(admonition). It is a fundamental ruling and its importance can
scarcely be exaggerated for the conduct of life, for the relations
between religion and morality, for the guidance of the individual
and of all mankind.

The question which of the commandments was the greatest
and all-comprehensive was of particular concern for Judaism.
The Jewish religion had increasingly developed into one of law.
The Jews regarded it as their distinction as the people of God
to have been given the Torah, the " law of Moses from Sinai,"
which determined their whole life, at once a joy and a burden.

It was therefore impossible for them to escape the question how the numerous precepts could be observed in daily life and how, despite human weakness, God's will could be carried out and salvation attained. The Pharisees' interpretation of the Mosaic law surrounded it with a protective fence, thus adding more and more precepts and prohibitions. Later it was reckoned there were 613 commandments, comprising 365 prohibitions (from the number of days in the year) and 248 positive precepts (allegedly from the number of members of the body). A distinction was drawn between greater and lesser, heavy and light commandments.

The scribe's question " Which commandment is the first of all " was therefore candid and serious. It echoes the passionate search of many of Jesus' compatriots for the way of salvation, which we have seen exemplified in the rich man (10:17).

Jesus speaks of love of God as the " first " commandment, but immediately adds love of the neighbor as second, according to Leviticus 19:18. No further explanation of this is given. As understood in the Old Testament, the " neighbor " was the fellow countryman and fellow Jew, but Leviticus 19:34 puts resident aliens on the same level. Later rabbinical exegesis generally limited the precept to Israelites and full proselytes, but there were others who maintained that the commandment extended to all humanity.

" There is no other commandment greater than these." This places love of the neighbor side by side with love of God as of equal importance, in fact brotherly love is pointed out as the domain in which love of God must be effectively realized and put to the test. In view of the scribe's conclusion, which Jesus approves, that this dual commandment is more than all the burnt offerings and sacrifices, that is, than all ritual worship of God, it must even be said that the practical expression of love for God by love of the neighbor represents the real kernel of Jesus' pronouncement.

The scribe reflects on Jesus' answer, recognizes its profound truth, and draws the conclusion that to love God and the neighbor in this way is more important than all the temple sacrifices. For this, Jesus gives him recognition and praise. "You are not far from the kingdom of God." Since the kingdom of God elsewhere appears as a reality brought about by God, which is already approaching (1:15), the meaning must be that this scribe has a share in it. He is on the best path to enter God's kingdom one day. Matthew omits this conclusion of the discussion, which is understandable, since he presents it as a controversy. Mark's attitude is more "ecumenical." Despite attacks elsewhere on the scribes (2:6; 3:22), despite the warning against them which he too transmits (12:38f.), there are individuals among them who are receptive to Jesus' preaching. The Church must not shut the door to them; good must be recognized wherever it is. Consequently the final remark that no one dared to ask Jesus any more questions does not refer specifically to this scene. It draws a final line under the foregoing controversies and at the same time forms an editorial transition to the next pericope in which Jesus himself propounds a question which throws light on the scribes' embarrassment.

THE QUESTION OF THE DAVIDIC SONSHIP OF THE MESSIAH (12:35–37a)

[35]*And as Jesus taught in the temple, he said, "How can the scribes say that the Christ is the son of David?* [36]*David himself, inspired by the Holy Spirit, declared, 'The Lord said to my Lord, Sit at my right hand, till I put thy enemies under thy feet.'* [37]*David himself calls him Lord; so how is he his son?"*

In all these controversies the evangelist is concerned not only with their actual content, but has a Christological aim. He is presenting Jesus as an unsurpassable teacher who gives permanently valid lessons to the Jews of that time and, what is even more important, to the Church. This pericope too contains a lesson of this kind, of the greatest importance for the Christian community because it concerns the person of Jesus himself. The way the early Church understood the question of the Davidic sonship of the Messiah which Jesus is dealing with here, and the answer which—unlike the silent scribes—it was able to give, is scarcely open to doubt within the framework of Mark's gospel. The Messiah whom the Church recognized in Jesus was the Son of God. Similarly, the cognate question on which exegetes are divided, whether it also regarded him as the son of David, must surely also be answered affirmatively. Genealogically, the Church acknowledged his Davidic sonship, but did not understand this in the sense of the Jewish messianic expectations, according to which the son of David would appear as an earthly king and liberator. Its Messiah indeed came of David's line and so fulfilled the ancient prophecy (2 Sam. 7:14; etc.). Yet he did not correspond in appearance and ministry to the national hope, but disappointed it while in fact far surpassing it. As well as being the son of David, he was the Son of God.

WARNING AGAINST THE SCRIBES (12:37b–40)

[37b]*And the great throng heard him gladly.* [38]*And in his teaching he said, " Beware of the scribes, who like to go about in long robes, and to have salutations in the market places* [39]*and the best seats in the synagogues and the places of honor at feasts,* [40]*who devour widows' houses and for a pretense make long prayers. They will receive the greater condemnation."*

The transition from the question about the son of David to the warning against the scribes is the evangelist's. The statement that the crowd gladly listened to Jesus could also form the conclusion of the previous pericope, since the reader expects some sort of reaction to the question Jesus has raised. But it was the scribes who had been called upon to answer. Instead, Mark sharply contrasts the attitude of the people with that of the scribes, who no longer come on the scene (cf. v. 34c). He has this tendency to dissociate the people from the leaders, who alone are responsible for rejecting and delivering up Jesus (cf. 11:32; 12:12; 14:1f.). The people acknowledges Jesus as teacher and the community must learn to listen as willingly to Jesus as the great crowd had done at that time, and to heed the doctrine that he was Messiah and Lord.

The scribes were very harshly criticized by Jesus at the end of these debates. From the tradition in Matthew, who compiles a multiple indictment of the scribes and Pharisees (chapter 23), and in Luke, who offers part of the same material in another context and in separate sayings against the Pharisees and teachers of the law (11:39–52), it is apparent that early on collections were made of Jesus' sharp censures of these influential people. There is no reason to doubt that Jesus, not only once but repeatedly, voiced criticism which won the deadly enmity of these circles. From this tradition Mark takes only a few telling shafts against the scribes; according to the other source, Jesus reproached them in similar terms to their faces. This fits the picture that his contemporaries formed of him as a prophet (cf. 6:15; 8:28); he was a fearless champion of God's cause against the influential and powerful among his people.

THE WIDOW'S MITE (12:41–44)

41And he sat down opposite the treasury, and watched the multitude putting money into the treasury. Many rich people put in large sums. ⁴²*And a poor widow came, and put in two copper coins, which make a penny.* ⁴³*And he called his disciples to him, and said to them, " Truly, I say to you, this poor widow has put in more than all those who are contributing to the treasury.* ⁴⁴*For they all contributed out of their abundance; but she out of her poverty has put in everything she had, her whole living."*

In the temple Court of the Women was a hall (the treasury) with thirteen trumpet-shaped receptacles for money offerings for various purposes, including voluntary gifts without special destination. Visitors to the temple did not insert the money themselves as we do into collection boxes, but handed it to the priests who put it in the receptacles as the donor decided. This explains how Jesus could see what the poor widow gave. She named the amount and its purpose to the priest and Jesus could hear her. In the circumstances she probably brought her very modest contribution as a voluntary gift without special destination, for which the thirteenth receptacle was reserved. This money was used to provide burnt offerings. The woman wanted only to do something for the glory of God. Alms for the poor were handed in elsewhere, or collected in a box.

The lesson for the disciples and consequently to the later community is plain. True piety is devotion to God; it means placing oneself totally at his disposal. This woman does not give of her superfluity, but out of her poverty and need. She gave away all that she had, perhaps (from the Greek expression) all that she had to live on that day. The *two* smallest Jewish coins show that she could still have reserved something for herself, but in fact she gave God everything and thereby gave herself. A person of this stamp will not fail to notice others in distress and share their last crust with them if need be. The widow loves God " with all her strength," which in the Jewish interpretation also meant with her whole earthly " property," all her possessions. There are non-Christian examples of high esteem for the inner disposition that prompts an action rather than the size of the gift or the mere scale of what is done. The Christian element can be discerned in the light of the great commandment, when a person gives himself lovingly in sacrifice to God, and, for his sake, to humanity.

The Great Apocalpytic Discourse (Chapter 13)

The controversies and discourses of Jesus in the temple are over. It might be expected that the drama of the Passion, towards which the whole gospel narrative is moving, would now unfold before its readers, and that chapter 12 would immediately be followed by chapter 14. It has been suggested that the great apocalyptic discourse in chapter 13, the longest speech in Mark, was perhaps only inserted into the gospel afterwards, in a situation (after A.D. 70) when the community was seriously disturbed by eschatological questions prompted by external events (destruction of Jerusalem) and by deceivers among the Christians themselves (fanatics who regarded the end of the world as imminent). This is possible but the assumption is quite unnecessary. The whole gospel, as we have seen, is orientated towards the community and its life. Time and time again by means of shorter passages of teaching addressed to the disciples, the evangelist has sought to convey a special lesson to the community for its faith and particular circumstances. Why should he not have brought together in one passage sayings and teaching of Jesus about the future, since, after all, Jesus' message was eminently one that concerned the future, an eschatological message? Why should he not have transposed these sayings of Jesus, who had always preached very urgently, prophetically, in a way that came home to his contemporaries, into the present situation of the Church community and applied them to an already different state of affairs? And what place in the gospel was more appropriate for this purpose than the end of the public ministry, before Jesus' voice fell silent in the Passion? Perhaps the link with the Passion must be regarded as an even closer one. Before the community moves in sympathy along its Lord's way of suffering and death, which it, too, has to follow in imitation of him (cf. 8 : 31–38), it is to hear its Lord's predictions, warnings, and reassurance collected and addressed to it, so that it has a better understanding of itself as Christ's Church to cope with the situation it is in.

PREDICTION OF THE DESTRUCTION OF THE TEMPLE (13 : 1–2)

¹And as he came out of the temple, one of his disciples said to him, " Look, Teacher, what wonderful stones and what wonderful buildings!" ²And Jesus said to him, " Do you see these great buildings? There will not be left here one stone upon another, that will not be thrown down."

The so-called temple of Herod in those days was a magnificent building. After the destruction of the first temple built by Solomon in 586 B.C., a new temple was not built until the years 520–515, after the return from the Babylonian exile under Zerubbabel, and was far from equal in splendor to the first (cf. Ezra 5–6). The Jews were proud of this temple despite their aversion to Herod the Great and his successors, and now, according to Jesus' words, it was to be destroyed. Scholars still dispute whether this represents a genuine prophecy on the part of Jesus, that is to say the actual prediction, or a *vaticinium ex eventu,* a statement after the event. Against the latter contention stands the fact that the destruction is not described as a fire, which is what really happened; on the other hand, the present text bears signs of Marcan shaping. It is even possible to state more precisely the " source " of the formulation—the already mentioned saying about the temple in 14:58. There can be no doubt that Jesus did utter a saying of this kind; it is, of course, in two parts. It speaks of destruction (the same term as in 13:2, " thrown down ") and also of the building of another temple, the spiritual temple of the community. Thus Jesus stands in a prophetic tradition, for even in earlier times prophets had foretold the ruin of the temple of Solomon. Similarly Jewish visionaries announced the destruction of Herod's temple before this actually occurred.

It is possible that Mark, too, was already looking back at the actual event; if that were so, the difficulties and questions raised in the community as well as the answer to them intended by the appended discourse, would be more easily explained. The catastrophe of Jerusalem and of the temple, which appeared to contemporaries as a terrible judgment of God, prompted the Christian community to question whether this was not perhaps the "beginning of the end," and apocalyptic fanatics sowed unrest in the community. Mark opposed this kind of deceptive talk, although he, too, was convinced that Christ's parousia would not be long delayed. But he also knew that Jesus had not indicated any definite date, but had intended simply to stress the need for constant vigilance and readiness. Historical events are always obscure and ambiguous; faith will hear God's voice in temporal events but will not venture to give precise answers as to what God's purpose is with them. Later Christian interpretations of the ruin of Jerusalem and of the temple, as though it meant that the Jewish people had been forever rejected and scattered throughout the world, are therefore unjustified, danger-ous, contrary, in fact, to the Christian faith and to Jesus' mind. They have contributed to the terrible persecutions of Jews. Jesus' saying and prophecy constitute, rather, a perpetual summons to personal reflection and continually renewed attention to the voice of God, even in the historical events which we are living through now.

THE APOCALYPTIC DISCOURSE: BEGINNING OF THE "SUFFERINGS" (13:3-13)

³And as he sat on the Mount of Olives opposite the temple, Peter and James and John and Andrew asked him privately, ⁴" Tell us, when will this be, and what will be the sign when these things are all to be accomplished?" ⁵And Jesus began to say to them, " Take heed that no one leads you astray. ⁶Many will come in my name, saying, ' I am he!' and they will lead many astray. ⁷And when you hear of wars and rumors of wars, do not be alarmed; this must take place, but the end is not yet. ⁸For nation will rise against nation, and kingdom against kingdom; there will be earthquakes in various places, there will be famines; this is but the beginning of the sufferings. ⁹But take heed of yourselves; for they will deliver you up to councils; and you will be beaten in synagogues; and you will stand before governors and kings for my sake, to bear testimony before them. ¹⁰And the gospel must first be preached to all nations. ¹¹And when they gospel must first be preached to all nations. ¹¹And when the bring you to trial and deliver you up, do not be anxious beforehand for it is not you who speak, but the Holy Spirit. ¹²And brother will deliver up brother to death, and the father his child, and children will rise against parents and have them put to death; ¹³and you will be hated by all for my name's sake. But he who endures to the end will be saved.

The scene which forms the introduction to the great parousia discourse is closely linked with the saying on the destruction of the temple; for the evangelist makes a point of noting that Jesus

D

is sitting on the Mount of Olives " opposite the temple," that is, with a view over the vast temple area, and that that is where his disciples question him.

The double question itself matches the questions that were occupying the community. The event inquired into is deliberately kept vague: " this," " these things." In its context the first question concerns the date of the destruction of the temple, the second widens the perspective, and the expression " to be accomplished " points to eschatological events. The coupling of the two questions, however, suggests that some relation is intended between the destruction of the temple and the eschatological fulfillment. Since the question concerns the " sign " of " these things " that are to be " accomplished," it is possible that appeal is being made to the expectation that the destruction of the temple constitutes this " sign," but in the form of a question : Is this expectation correct or is there another " sign "? The double " this " and " these things " occurs again in verses 29 and 30. According to verse 29, it can be " known " that the parousia (or Christ at the parousia) is " at the very gates," and according to verse 30, " this generation " will not pass before " all these things " take place. In his own mind the evangelist must have regarded the destruction of the temple or the mysterious " desolating sacrilege " of verse 14 as some kind of a portent or prefiguration.

Jesus' discourse begins by listing things which must indeed take place but do not yet mean theend. The two imperatives stand out as its articulations: " Take heed that no one leads you astray!" (v. 5); and " Take heed to yourselves!" (v. 9). Deceivers will appear, claiming themselves to be the eschatological saviour, the parousia Christ. To what extent such people did appear in the community or on its fringes is impossible to say; yet the warning against " false Christs and false prophets " is repeated (vv. 21f.), in conjunction with the theme " But take heed; I have told you all things beforehand " (v. 23). This sounds like a repetition and conclusion of the initial warning. It might well be inferred that the community had in fact known such people.

It is even more important to take heed to oneself. This warning (v. 9) introduces a new description, which presupposes Jewish circumstances and directly concerns the disciples. They will be delivered for trial, according to the Greek expression, before Jewish local courts, which also had the right to inflict the penalty of scourging. They will even be dragged before Roman governors and "kings," that is, Roman vassal princes, for Jesus' sake. " To bear testimony before them " need not refer to the testimony of faith borne by those brought before the court (as at Mt. 10:18); it can also mean: as testimony against them at the divine judgment (cf. 6:11). But as transition to verse 10 the thought seems rather to be that their confession of faith serves the proclamation of the gospel. Then in verse 10 the vista widens: the gospel must first be preached to all nations. This is in harmony with the universalist attitude of the evangelist, who understands that the Church is " a house of prayer for all the nations " (11:17), and with his thought that the gospel will be preached in the whole world (cf. 14:9). The word " first," like the expressions " the end is not yet " (v. 7) and " beginning of the sufferings " (v. 8), introduces a retarding factor in the presentation, but does not suppress the imminent expectation, because the evangelist is thinking only of the world of the Roman empire, which at that time was the whole known world.

In verse 11, which links up with the trial situation of verse 9, a motive of reassurance is introduced, the assistance of the Holy Spirit. It will not be the disciples who are the real speakers, but the Holy Spirit, who thus appears in a role which also figures in the Johannine Paraclete sayings, as helper and advocate in the law courts (cf. Jn. 16:8-11).

Linked by the keyword " deliver up," two further descriptions follow. Even members of the same family will bring one another to trial and deliver them up to death. It is clear that betrayal and hatred because of faith is meant; the disciples will be hated by all for Jesus' name's sake.

The grim passage ends, however, with a word of comfort. The exhortation to " endure " is frequently found in the apocalypses, as in Daniel 12 : 12 where we read : " Blessed is he who waits [endures] . . ." This is an apocalyptic mode of thought: God brings the elect safely through tribulation. In Mark the sense is different: He who endures to the end, that is, in this context, who remains faithful even to death and martyrdom, will attain salvation.

THE GREAT TRIBULATION (13 :14–23)

14" But when you see the desolating sacrilege set up where it ought not to be (let the reader understand), then let those who are in Judea flee to the mountains; 15let him who is on the housetop not go down, nor enter his house, to take anything away; 16and let him who is in the field not turn back to take his mantle. 17And alas for those who are with child and for those who give suck in those days! 18Pray that it may not happen in winter. 19For in those days there will be such tribulation as has not been from the beginning of the creation which God created until now, and never will be. 20And if the Lord had not shortened the days, no human being would be saved; but for the sake of the elect, whom he chose, he shortened the days. 21And then if anyone says to you, ' Look, here is the Christ! ' or ' Look, there he is! ' do not believe it. 22False Christs and false prophets will arise and show signs and wonders, to lead astray, if possible, the elect. 23But take heed; I have told you all things beforehand.

If an eschatological interpretation is acceptable here, this passage is a glimpse into the future, into the period immediately before the end, expressed by the traditional methods of apocalyptic description. If, however, one decides to explain the section as referring to contemporary history, and assume that the destruction of the temple has already taken place, then the section fits meaningfully into the discourse as a whole. The terrible event is unfolded before the Christians' eyes in the stylistic form of a prediction, and using traditional apocalyptic language. At the same time it is said that they pay no heed to false prophets (vv. 21f.). Jesus has foretold it all (v. 23) but had not intimated that the parousia was to follow at once. Only at verse 24 does the gaze really turn to the future; but in accordance with the expectation that Christ will soon return, which is shared by Mark himself, and for which the destruction of the temple (with the abomination which causes desolation) is yet another sign, a significant portent, it is said in more general terms, " But in those days, after that tribulation . . ." The parousia does not necessarily have to follow immediately, yet it is envisaged by the evangelist as not very far distant. This view has much to recommend it; but it is very doubtful whether any part was played in it by an " apocalyptic broadsheet " which is supposed to have appeared earlier, then to have come into circulation again about A.D. 70, and to have been exploited by Christian fanatics. We have no evidence in antiquity for any such modern proceeding. The remarkable description in verses 14c–20 which was certainly based on some source will probably have to be explained in some other way.

The expression " abomination that makes desolate " occurs in three passages of the Book of Daniel (9:27; 11:31; 12:11), where it refers to the setting up of an altar of Zeus in the temple of Jerusalem by Antiochus Epiphanes in 168 B.C. "Abomination " in the Old Testament signifies an idol and then pagan abominations generally. The " desolation " in Daniel 12:11 means the profanation of the temple, but according to Daniel 9:26f. can also include the destruction of the city: " The people of the prince who is to come shall destroy the city and the sanctuary." The evangelist must very likely have used some prophetic, apocalyptic description, which gave an indirect warning against some profaner of the temple ("where he ought not to be "). The injunction " Let the reader understand " must be the evangelist's own, and if he and the readers were already looking back on the destruction of Jerusalem and the temple, it could bear the meaning: Understand correctly, the prophecy has been fulfilled. In that case the devastator would be the Roman, perhaps the conquerer himself, Titus. But complete certainty cannot be had.

The injunction to flee to the hills is an ancient theme. When the religious wars broke out under King Antiochus IV, the Maccabees fled to the hills with the Jews who were faithful to the law (1 Macc. 2:28), but this, of course, was in order to assemble for battle. In Mark's source material, the metaphor of flight was probably only intended to suggest the great tribulation. The urgency of the flight and consequent gravity of the distress are emphasized by two other images drawn from Palestinian conditions. Anyone who is on the roof—the flat roof was a favorite resort—is not to go down but, for example if the house is on a hillside, is to flee at once and not go into the house again to fetch anything. Any delay may be fatal. Those in the fields are not to return home, not even to get their mantle— and this in Palestine, where the cold nights make a cloak indispensable. A lament is expressed for pregnant women and nursing mothers, hampered by their condition or responsibility for the baby. Finally, they are to pray that the flight will not happen in winter, when the rivers are swollen and make flight difficult. These are not instructions to be taken literally, but imagery depicting the calamitous situation in ready-made expressions.

Thus the warning "Let him not turn back" may echo Lot's flight from Sodom (cf. Gen. 19:17).

The meaning of this whole passage becomes even clearer when the great tribulation is mentioned. The text directly echoes Daniel 12:1 from which the idea of an unparalleled time of tribulation before the end entered the apocalyptic writings. It is presented in ever new imagery with catastrophes, wars, plagues, extraordinary events in nature. These words certainly exaggerate the distress of the Jewish War, but if it is a prophecy, what was to come could deliberately be described by such apocalyptic features. The next statement likewise simply serves to emphasize the extreme distress. For the "shortening" of the time is likewise a typical apocalyptic motif: "for the age is hastening fast to its end" (4 Ezra 4:26).

Mark has taken over all these images and motifs, like the seer of Revelation whose descriptions are even more luxuriant. We can and must abandon them in our world view, but the essential idea that Mark seeks to convey vividly by them, namely the somber and threatening element in history which is a feature of this world, remains. The injunction to flee must not be taken literally; that would contradict the preceding command to endure steadfastly (v. 13). The metaphor of flight also suggests watchfulness and resolute action.

A vigilant and critical attitude is also required, because false prophets will come on the scene (vv. 21f.). External misfortune will be intensified by the interior distress of confusing talk and misleading actions. For these pseudo-Christs and pseudo-prophets will perform "signs and wonders" in order to deceive God's elect. This warning was probably given because of actual cases in the evangelist's time. The exclamations "Look, here is the Christ!" or "Look, there he is!" suggest Christian fanatics who were convinced the parousia had come.

The concluding warning shows that confusion, inner uncertainty, weakness of faith, are even more dangerous for Christians than external misfortune and persecution. Jesus' words " I have told you beforehand " in the actual context of course serve to counteract the bewildering and deceptive features of the events of that time, but they retain their power to strengthen, for deceitful talk and dangerous propaganda perpetually threaten to distort the view of faith. The ambiguous twilight is also part of the world of history, whose course is accompanied by a sinister power of evil, but can never escape the will and saving plan of God.

THE PAROUSIA OF THE SON OF MAN (13:24–27)

[24]" *But in those days, after that tribulation, the sun will be darkened, and the moon will not give its light,* [25]*and the stars will be falling from heaven, and the powers in the heavens will be shaken.* [26]*And then they will see the Son of man coming in clouds with great power and glory.* [27]*And then he will send out the angels, and gather his elect from the four winds, from the ends of the earth to the ends of heaven.*

What is here described is not the " end of the world," but a cosmic drama which uses a mode of representation current at that time in order to focus attention on the parousia. Sun, moon, and stars are spoken of as naïvely as they are in the account of the creation. But they no longer perform their service now; the sun is darkened, the moon no longer shines, the stars fall from the sky—all statements which echo Old Testament passages (Is. 13:10; 34:4). These metaphors do not depict a judgment, they merely prepare for the great event to which the whole scene leads up.

" And then " this awaited event occurs: " They will see the

Son of man coming in clouds . . ." These clouds "in which" the Son of man comes in the sight of all, were also a recognized symbol. Like the whole passage, they are taken from the vision in Daniel 7:13: "I saw in the night visions, and behold, with the clouds of heaven there came one like a son of man." There, this heavenly figure is led before the throne of the Most High; here, however, the Son of man comes from heaven. The Christian use and reinterpretation of the Danielic vision is unmistakable. The biblical symbolic language is retained, because only so can the transcendent event be expressed; but a new level of understanding has opened out for the Christian Church through the resurrection of its Lord. The Son of man to whom, according to Daniel 7:14, power is then given by God is Jesus Christ already established in his glory with God. At his coming (the parousia) he will manifest himself as ruler, and gather his community around him.

The parousia stands, of course, in very close connection with other expectations for the future, the resurrection and the judgment, which were firmly supported by Jesus; it is, as it were, merely a Christological reinterpretation of the actions of God which bring about the consummation. It is dangerous to lessen the universal, cosmic, and eschatological dimension of the kingdom of God announced by Jesus. For the early Church's consciousness of its faith, the coming kingdom which Jesus proclaimed is brought by its risen Lord; conversely, it can be said that this kingdom brings Jesus himself as the one who represented it and realized it symbolically by his earthly ministry. Consequently, parousia and the coming kingdom of God were bound up inseparably for the early Church, and its hope in the kingdom finds its firm expression and sure support in the affirmation of the parousia.

THE PARABLE OF THE FIG TREE
AND THE QUESTION OF THE HOUR (13:28–32)

²⁸*" From the fig tree learn its lesson: as soon as its branch becomes tender and puts forth its leaves, you know that summer is near. ²⁹So also, when you see these things taking place, you know that he is near, at the very gates. ³⁰Truly, I say to you, this generation will not pass away before all these things take place. ³¹Heaven and earth will pass away, but my words will not pass away. ³²But of that day or that hour no one knows, not even the angels in heaven, nor the Son, but only the Father.*

After the description of the parousia, the question which was the starting point of the entire discourse (v. 4) is taken up again. The parable of the fig tree is easily understood from the image itself. After the rainy season the fig tree puts out particularly big, sap-filled leaves, visible from a distance, an unmistakable sign of the sudden onset of the Palestinian summer. Verse 29 applies the parable to " this " [RSV: " he "]—obviously to what has just been described. The evangelist is referring back to the events of the parousia, for these, or the perfect kingdom of God which they bring about, or even the parousia Christ himself, can be recognized thereby to be standing " at the very gates." Jesus certainly told a parable of this kind, but it may be conjectured that its original meaning was different. Luke has preserved a similar parable which speaks of observable signs, particularly weather signs (12:54ff.). But there it is a question of things that can be seen in Jesus himself and his ministry. Jesus reproaches the " hypocrites " for being able to interpret the appearance of earth and sky but not " the present time." In the context of Jesus' message of the kingdom of God that can only mean that in his ministry, in his preaching and teaching, his cures and exorcisms the approaching kingdom of God is being heralded in signs, and calls for conversion and faith here and now. For Mark and his community, who are awaiting their Lord's coming, attention turns to the intermediate period, which for them is the present moment and time of decision.

The imminent expectation is even clearer in the saying that "this generation" will not pass away before "all these things" take place (v. 31). The expression "all these things" here (as in v. 4b) denotes the whole series of events including the parousia. The saying is akin to Mark 9:1, perhaps was developed from it, at all events is identical in meaning: some contemporaries of Jesus will live to see those events. "This generation" will not have passed away by then. In Jesus' preaching "this generation" is often referred to, always in an unfavorable sense, as a sinful, "adulterous" generation, unfaithful to God (Mk. 8:12, 38; 9:19). But it does not mean the human race or Judaism in general, but the particular generation at that time, as the evidence for the use of the word overwhelmingly shows.

The next saying (v. 31) affirms solemnly but quite generally that Jesus' words will not pass away, using an impressive contrast with heaven and earth which will pass away. This first term of the comparison has no independent meaning: it is not emphasizing the end of the world; it simply serves to underline that what Jesus says is irrevocable. Here, too, an earlier saying must probably have been shaped to fit the context and the evangelist's intention; for the same motif is met with in the saying, "But it is easier for heaven and earth to pass away than for one dot of the law to become void" (Lk. 16:17; cf. Mt. 5:18), which, of course, inculcates the holiness and validity of the law. Perhaps Mark's source had already linked verse 30 and verse 31 by the catchword "pass away." But the statement in verse 31 retains its force even independently. By applying it to different instances, the early Church proclaimed its faith that Jesus' words remain true and binding, whether in moral precept or prophetic promise. They are not to be interpreted with slavish literalness (that cannot be the meaning of the " dot of the law," either) but are to be understood in their spirit and applied to the particular situation at any given time.

The very strong mode of expression that no one, not even the angels or the Son, knows the day or the hour has always attracted attention. There is no real Christological difficulty in the " nescience " of the earthly Jesus, if the incarnation of the divine Logos is taken seriously, and it is of minor importance to decide whether Jesus referred to himself as " the Son " in this absolute way or was only so designated by the early Church. Jesus' reserved way of speaking about himself was legitimately developed by the early Church after his resurrection to the stage of explicit utterance, as we have already seen in the parable of the wicked husbandmen with its mention of the son. The decisive import of the verse, however, that knowledge of the last things is reserved to God alone, has a firm basis in Jesus' preaching.

Exhortation to Watchfulness (13:33-37)

[33]" *Take heed, watch and pray; for you do not know when the time will come.* [34]*It is like a man going on a journey, when he leaves home and puts his servants in charge, each with his work, and commands the doorkeeper to be on the watch.* [35]*Watch therefore—for you do not know when the master of the house will come, in the evening, or at midnight, or at cockcrow, or in the morning—*[36]*lest he come suddenly and find you asleep.* [37]*And what I say to you I say to all: Watch.*"

The aim of the evangelist here was not to convey disclosures about the future, but to provide the people with a Christian attitude for the present. For this purpose he uses a parable which Jesus had once told, as he had the parable of the weather signs, in order to prepare his hearers for what was to come and to stimulate them to respond to his message in the way called for there and then. Once again the early Church has applied Jesus' parable to its own situation in the intermediate period between Easter and parousia.

In its present form the parable has some remarkable features. If the warning to be watchful is the sole point, everything hangs on the doorkeeper, who has to admit his master on his return. Mention of the other servants and the tasks assigned to them is really superfluous; they appear as minor characters with no particular part to play in the master's homecoming. But if we think of the community, it is clear that the evangelist has a purpose. The servants stand for all the faithful, each with their own task assigned to them by Christ, the master of the house, and all equally exhorted to vigilance. That is plain and unmistakable in the final words, " And what I say to you I say to all : Watch." The disciples to whom Jesus is talking represent all future believers; the same vigilant attitude is required of all.

The Passion, Death, and Resurrection of Jesus (14:1—16:8)

The gospels have been described as " a Passion narrative with detailed introduction." If that applies to all the gospels, it is particularly true of Mark. The whole presentation, especially in the second part after the scene at Caesarea Philippi, is orientated towards the events of the Passion in which God's saving plan is fulfilled. After the initiation of the disciples into the mystery of Jesus' death, his last ministry in the Jewish capital, and the great apocalyptic discourse for the community, the evangelist now at last begins the narrative of these events. His language remains unemotional. Some of the terrible things which later Christians have pictured with profound emotion, such as the scourging or nailing to the cross, receive only brief mention. They were well known to people of that age as measures by which a harsh justice was carried out, and affected their feelings less than the reasons which lay behind Jesus' condemnation and execution, or the deep mystery that the Son of God had to take upon himself such incomprehensible suffering. This profounder aspect of his sufferings finds expression particularly in Gethsemane, when Jesus in agony of soul passes in anticipation through the abyss of mortal suffering and death, and in his last words on the cross, when he cries his utter dereliction, his apparent remoteness from God. At the same time all this is seen in the light of scriptural prophecy which is fulfilled in him and which he himself consciously intends to fulfill. The deeper causes of these events are disclosed chiefly in the trial of Jesus, not as a matter of mere historical interest, but in order to make clear the driving forces, the unjust accusation, the malice of the Jewish leaders, and the weakness of the Roman judge. Humanly speaking, a monstrous judicial error; viewed in relation to God, an inevitable conflict, in which Jesus became involved for the sake of his mission and claim, yet a necessary one if he was to fulfill his mission.

We may divide the story of the Passion according to Mark into the following sections: (1) From the opponents' plot to Jesus' arrest (14:1–52); (2) the proceedings before the Sanhedrin and the trial before Pilate (14:53—15:15); (3) Passion, cross, and tomb (15:16—16:8).

The Opponents' Plot, the Anointing in Bethany, the Last Supper,
Gethsemane and Arrest (14 : 1–52)

The first part of the Passion narrative is opened by the priests'
plot, assisted by the offer of the traitor Judas Iscariot to betray
him. Mark has inserted into this unit of tradition the account of
the anointing in Bethany (14:3–9). In this way the reader is not
only made familiar with the external situation but put into the
right frame of mind. Jesus foresees his death and understands it
as the accomplishment of the way which leads to his glorifica-
tion and the victory of the gospel. Thus a contrasting picture
emerges; against a dark background, a bright promise stands
out. The last hours spent with his disciples likewise show Jesus
as foreseeing and determining everything, as he had done at the
entry into Jerusalem (14:12–17, cf. 11:1–6), knowing about the
treachery and the death allotted to him (14:18–21) and accom-
plishing during the meal with his disciples a profoundly significant action which points both to his death and to the coming
kingdom. The account of the institution of the Eucharist, which
becomes of the highest importance for the Church after Jesus'
death, is so arranged in the framework of Mark's Passion narrative that after the relation between the Eucharist and Jesus'
death is made clear, its eschatological symbolism is brought out
(14:25), and this again is a vista full of promise. The walk to
the Mount of Olives then leads deeper into the dark mystery of
the death and is an immediate introduction to the Passion:
prophecy of the dispersion of the disciples and Peter's denial,
Jesus' loneliness and mortal agony in the Garden of Gethsemane,
finally the approach of the traitor and Jesus' arrest. All the disciples flee (14:50), even, also, a young man who is nearby
(14:52); totally abandoned by his own, Jesus is led away and
enters on his path of suffering.

THE PLOT OF THE JEWISH LEADERS (14:1-2)

¹It was now two days before the Passover and the Feast of Unleavened Bread. And the chief priests and the scribes were seeking how to arrest him by stealth, and kill him; ²for they said, "Not during the feast, lest there be a tumult of the people."

The time indication "after two days" (as the Greek text reads) does not connect up with a previously related event but looks forward, and means two days before the feast day. The latter is designated here by the double expression, "the Passover and the Feast of Unleavened Bread." The Passover was only the first day of the festival week, or, more exactly, the evening on which the paschal lamb was eaten. The date was fixed as the night of the first full moon after the spring equinox (= 14/15 Nisan) and was carefully observed. On the day before, all leavened bread had to be removed from the house (cf. 14:12) and during the whole festival week only unleavened bread was eaten. A session of the Sanhedrin with an official condemnation of Jesus to death is not indicated; it is only with Matthew that it is represented as such (26:3f.). Mark names only the chief priests and the scribes (without the "elders"; cf. 8:31; 11:27) as the real adversaries of Jesus (as at 10:33; 11:18).

The explanatory remark in verse 2 presents a certain difficulty in this respect, since their calculation seems to bear on the time, the suitable moment. The fear that there might be a disturbance during the Passover was not without foundation; for in fact at this great festival, when messianic expectations were rife and national feeling easily spread among the thousands of pilgrims, there were repeated uprisings. On the other hand, the emphasis on the intention to arrest Jesus by stealth becomes intelligible against the background of an injunction of the Mishnah that certain malefactors were to be executed publicly at a pilgrimage festival (Sanhedrin XI, 3).

As before during the days in Jerusalem, the evangelist is at pains to distinguish between the Jewish leaders and the people at large. The former not only methodically plan his death, but are ready to use any means. They are afraid of a popular tumult less, perhaps, because it might thwart their intention than because they foresee its political consequences, the intervention of the Romans and the loss of their last vestige of power (cf. Jn. 11:47–53). For Mark, however, it is part of the mysterious lot of the Son of man to be delivered up through stealth and malignity, secrecy and treachery, and to be arrested like a bandit in the darkness of the night (cf. 14:43–49).

THE ANOINTING AT BETHANY AND THE TRAITOR'S OFFER (14:3–11)

³*And while he was at Bethany in the house of Simon the leper, as he sat at table, a woman came with an alabaster jar of ointment of pure nard, very costly, and she broke the jar and poured it over his head.* ⁴*But there were some who said to themselves indignantly, " Why was the ointment thus wasted?* ⁵*For this ointment might have been sold for more than three hundred denarii, and given to the poor." And they reproached her.* ⁶*But Jesus said, " Let her alone; why do you trouble her? She has done a beautiful thing to me.* ⁷*For you always have the poor with you, and whenever you will, you can do good to them; but you will not always have me.* ⁸*She has done what she could; she has anointed my body beforehand for burying.* ⁹*And truly, I say to you, wherever the gospel is preached in the whole world, what she has done will be told in memory of her."* ¹⁰*Then Judas*

Iscariot, who was one of the twelve, went to the chief priests in order to betray him to them. ¹¹And when they heard it they were glad, and promised to give him money. And he sought an opportunity to betray him.

The story of the anointing at Bethany was related at an early date in the Church. It is firmly linked with the place already mentioned at Jesus' entry into Jerusalem (cf. 11:1, 11f.), a village not quite two miles away on the eastern shoulder of the Mount of Olives. The style has Semitic features and the ideas are likewise explained by the Jewish mentality. There is therefore no reason to doubt its authenticity. Only its chronological place is not entirely certain. The Marcan account is certainly older and nearer the original.

Simon " the leper," probably because he had once been one (actual leprosy cannot be meant), gives Jesus a banquet. The guests reclined on cushions around the table. Jesus did not refuse invitations of this kind but women were permitted only to serve on such occasions. Consequently it was unusual for a woman to come in during the meal, and to anoint Jesus' head with precious oil was a mark of high esteem and honor. The oil was produced from the Indian nard plant, or, rather, from its roots; this explains the high price of 300 denarii (300 days' pay for a laborer at that time). The indignation of those present at this " waste " is understandable. Jesus defends the woman from these reproaches and says things which are the reason why the Church remembered the incident and continued to relate it.

For the Christian community, the woman had paid Jesus an honor which, after Easter, Christians too wanted to show him, an honor which was his due as the Son of God. It is, we may say, the foundation of a ritual veneration of Jesus, of a liturgical worship which is due to the Lord put to death shamefully but raised from the dead by God. History shows that the early

Church, notwithstanding the duty of charitable service of the poor, which it endeavored to fulfill, did not neglect liturgical worship of its Lord, not indeed in isolation, like a Hellenic cult fraternity, but nevertheless as an expression of union with its crucified and risen Lord, from which it drew strength for its ministry in the world and to endure affliction and persecution.

In dark contrast is Judas Iscariot's scheme to betray Jesus to the chief priests. He is expressly described as " one of the twelve " (in Greek, even more pointedly, the definite article is used: " the one of the twelve "—an echo of that enigma which the early Church could never fathom, that one of the closest circle of disciples could turn traitor, and which is still clearly perceptible in the Gospel of St. John (6:70f.; 13:21). The early Church already tried to understand his motives, and later reflection tried even more. With Mark, the motive of avarice and covetousness is only hinted at, for the chief priests themselves offer the traitor money. In Matthew, Judas bargains with them about the price, and the thirty pieces of silver recall the words of the prophet Zechariah 11:12. In John, Judas is branded as a dishonest administrator of the common funds, as a " thief " (12:6). What motives actually impelled the man (perhaps disappointed messianic hopes among others) can no longer be determined. For Mark, the sad observation suffices that he sought a favorable opportunity to betray Jesus, allying himself with the chief priests who were plotting Jesus' death.

PREPARATIONS FOR THE PASSOVER (14:12-16)

[12] *And on the first day of Unleavened Bread, when they sacrificed the Passover lamb, his disciples said to him, " Where will you have us go and prepare for you to eat the Passover? "* [13] *And he sent two of his disciples, and said to them, " Go into the city,*

and a man carrying a jar of water will meet you; follow him,
¹⁴and wherever he enters, say to the householder, ' The Teacher
says, Where is my guest room, where I am to eat the Passover
with my disciples?' ¹⁵And he will show you a large upper room
furnished and ready; there prepare for us." ¹⁶And the disciples
set out and went to the city, and found it as he had told them;
and they prepared the Passover.

It is historically certain that Jesus was put to death on a Friday,
probably in the year 30 or in 33; it was the " day of preparation "
for the sabbath (Mk. 15:42 par.; cf. Jn. 19:31, 42). Unfortunately
we do not know on what day the Passover (the night of 14/15
Nisan) fell, and therefore whether Jesus was crucified on 14 or
15 Nisan.

The insertion of the events of the Last Supper in the Passover
framework might be due to a theological intention, namely that
of regarding Jesus' institution as the new Christian Passover,
as it were a transformation of the Jewish Passover. In fact, the
Passover features appear only before and after the institution of
the Eucharist, clearly in the pericope regarding the preparations
for the meal, and then, less definitely, in the brief remark that
the disciples went out to the Mount of Olives " when they had
sung a hymn." This singing fits the pattern of a Passover meal
(second part of the Hallel psalms after eating the Passover lamb
and drinking the third cup of wine). The account of the preparation for the Passover, however, has peculiar features and, from
the point of view of the history of the tradition, can scarcely
belong to its oldest stratum.

The similarity of this story to the preparation for Jesus' entry
into Jerusalem (11:1–6) has long been noticed. There we observed
that miraculous foreknowledge and sovereign dominion were
attributed to Jesus. Here, too, the same features appear, even
more markedly. Jesus sends two of his disciples in advance and

tells them beforehand that they will meet a water carrier in the city and they only need to follow him to find the house where they can prepare for the Passover evening. The householder already knows about it and has a suitable large upper room already equipped for Jesus' celebration with his disciples. The disciples only need to make the immediate preparations, namely lay the table with things required for the Passover meal: the "bitter herbs" which in accordance with Exodus 12:8 formed part of the meal, also the dish with fruit purée, which by its red color recalled the mud which the Israelites had once had to make into bricks in Egypt. Finally, sufficient wine had to be available, because four (or perhaps at that time only three) cups were ritually prescribed. Not the slightest mention is made here or later of the most important item required at this sacred meal, the Passover lamb, which had to be slaughtered beforehand in the temple and was then eaten at home by the small Passover community (which, as far as numbers are concerned, could well have consisted of Jesus and his disciples). Is that a sign that the early Church did not really know for certain whether Jesus celebrated a Jewish Passover meal with his disciples or not? Luke 22:15 cannot decide the question either.

The evangelist's chief aim is to show how Jesus, who knows what God has ordained, deliberately prepares for the last hours he will spend with his disciples. The two disciples whom he sends (Peter and John, according to Lk. 22:8) find everything as he had told them. That is the point, not the details.

The Prophecy of the Betrayal (14:17–21)

¹⁷*And when it was evening he came with the twelve.* ¹⁸*And as they were at table eating, Jesus said, " Truly, I say to you, one of you will betray me, one who is eating with me." * ¹⁹*They began*

to be sorrowful, and to say to him one after another, " Is it I? "
[20]He said to them, " It is one of the twelve, one who is dipping
bread in the same dish with me. [21]For the Son of man goes as it
is written of him, but woe to that man by whom the Son of man
is betrayed! It would have been better for that man if he had not
been born."

By Jewish reckoning, the Passover evening began at sunset. Then
the domestic Passover celebration consisted of a ritual meal
which recalled the deliverance of the fathers from bondage in
Egypt. This saving event was to be re-enacted by the rite, consequently one part of it was the Passover *haggadah*, an explanation, by the person presiding, of the meaning of the meal with
paschal lamb, unleavened bread and bitter herbs. Each generation
was to look upon itself as having gone out from Egypt. Seriousness, joy, and hope mingled in this unique festival. But for the
Christian community, the deliverance of Israel was replaced by
the thought of redemption by the blood of Christ; " For Christ,
our paschal lamb, has been sacrificed " as Paul writes (1 Cor. 5 : 7).

Mark presents the framework of the Passover celebration but
fills it with new content. Whether the Last Supper was a Passover meal or not, what was important for the Church was what
was special and novel introduced by Jesus. What he said and did
at this last gathering with his disciples was retained and retold,
some things merely as reminiscence, recollection, but the most
important, the institution of the Eucharist, as a constant memorial, actually to effect communion with the Lord who had gone
to death and would come again one day (cf. 1 Cor. 11 : 26).
Mark constructs his concise account so deliberately that the
deepest darkness, the betrayal by one of the twelve, is followed
by the institution of the Eucharist, and this again culminates in
the prospect of the coming kingdom of God.

By a short transition (v. 17), the evangelist links the preceding narrative with the Last Supper. At a late hour, that is, in the evening, Jesus comes with the twelve. The disciples are introduced under this designation because they represent the Church and because Judas is emphasized then with sorrowful perplexity as " one of you " (v. 18), " one of the twelve " (v. 20).

Jesus' announcement refers to a passage in the Psalms, " Even my bosom friend in whom I trusted, who ate of my bread, has lifted his heel against me " (Ps. 41:9). For the early Church, even the betrayal of Jesus loses something of its incomprehensibility through scripture (cf. Jn. 17:12). Deeply moved, the disciples start to ask one after another, " Is it I? " According to Mark, Jesus does not unmask the traitor, either by saying anything to him directly (Mt. 26:25), or by a sign to another disciple (Jn. 13:25f.). He simply reiterates his prediction and emphasizes to all the disciples the dreadful character of that deed by a " woe."

Theologically, the saying about the Son of man is the focal point for Mark. The Son of man " goes," enters on the way ordained for him. It is pointless to look for some particular passage of scripture which announces this fate, as in 8:31, although for the early Church the prophecy of the atoning Servant of God of Isaiah 53 will have formed its background. There is no reflection on that here. It is enough that it is ordained for him, his hour must be fulfilled, he " is betrayed into the hands of sinners " (14:41). The woe is an old prophetic stylistic form of warning and threat to express the infamy and danger to salvation of such an action. The stern statement " It would have been better for that man if he had not been born " does not directly declare the eternal damnation of the traitor; it is a Jewish turn of phrase, of which other examples are extant, a hyperbole similar to the saying in 9:42. But the threat of eternal judgment lies behind it (cf. Jn. 17:12); hence the horror at Judas' action and the thought of the perdition to which " that man " has exposed himself.

THE INSTITUTION OF THE EUCHARIST (14:22–25)

²²And as they were eating, he took bread, and blessed, and broke it, and gave it to them, and said, " Take; this is my body." *²³And he took a cup, and when he had given thanks he gave it to them, and they all drank of it.* *²⁴And he said to them, " This is my blood of the covenant, which is poured out for many.* *²⁵Truly, I say to you, I shall not drink again of the fruit of the vine until that day when I drink it new in the kingdom of God."*

The new opening " And as they were eating " (cf. v. 18) reveals that Mark has inserted an originally independent account into his narrative. The prophecy of the betrayal and the institution of the Eucharist need not therefore have followed one another immediately; it also shows that not everything is reported about this last meal of Jesus. But the action which Jesus then performs and which Mark relates in simple words was of the greatest importance for the early Church. Everything we know about it shows that from the beginning it regularly celebrated the Eucharist or " Lord's Supper " (1 Cor. 11:20); Paul attests this and appeals to the tradition already handed down to him (1 Cor. 11:23).

The institution of the Eucharist involved an action performed by Jesus and accompanied by certain words. Mark uses five verbs to describe Jesus' actions in regard to the bread, and each of these verbs merits attention. He " takes " bread, lifts it, as the person presiding over the company at table, just as the head of the household had to do at every meal, to pronounce a blessing over the bread. Here, however, it is not at the beginning, but during the meal. At the Passover meal, the moment for this might have been when the main course began after the Passover *haggadah,* the first part of the Hallel (singing of Ps. 113-114) and the drinking of the second cup. Yet at other festival meals, too, there was a preliminary course before the main meal. In conjunction with what follows, the " taking " of the bread signifies Jesus' intention of doing something special and new.

He at once pronounces the blessing prayer over the bread, as the father of the house always did among the Jews, a thanksgiving for God's gift, at that time still perhaps freely improvised, later a fixed grace. Jesus therefore was following Jewish custom, but may even here have expressed ideas of his own, for example, his special relation with the Father (later, of course, the " Our Father " became the Church's grace before meals at its eucharistic celebration). Only with the cup does Mark use the Greek word " to thank," which later, as " Eucharist," came to denote the whole sacred action.

The two verbs mentioned (participles in the Greek) lead to a first main statement: He broke the bread. The unleavened loaves at the Passover meal (" matzos ") consisted of big flat slices; Jewish bread generally was like that, sometimes tough slices that had to be broken or torn. What Jesus did was therefore nothing out of the ordinary, and no deeper symbolism is to be seen in it, for example, an allusion to his violent death. The breaking of the bread in fact has to be linked with the next main statement, the " giving," and understood as a unified action: Jesus distributes the broken or separated fragments to his disciples. In the Jewish view all who received and ate a piece of bread from the paterfamilias shared in the blessing which he had spoken. First he distributed the fragments, then he himself took a piece and began to eat; this was the sign for all to eat, that the meal had begun. But we are not told that Jesus himself ate some of this bread which he distributed. On the contrary, he clearly omitted to do so, for he expressly invites the disciples, " Take " (Matthew adds, " eat "), which shows that he did not give the usual sign by eating himself. At every meal, the Jewish rite itself, the breaking and distribution of the bread, emphasized the fellowship of those at table, and Jesus' special action underlined this even further. All eat of the one bread and this communal relationship becomes one of the basic ideas in the primitive Christian understanding of the eucharistic celebration.

The special character of the bread thus distributed, however, could only be expressed and conveyed to those at table by speech (" and he said "), communicated as something new and unheard of. The words over the bread belong inseparably and inescapably to the action, but at the same time are themselves explained by the action: " This is my body." It has been suggested that this is a word of explanation like the words spoken in the Passover *haggadah* over the bread: " Behold, the bread of affliction which our fathers ate who went out from the lands of the Egyptians," or, " This is the bread of affliction." But in this the repetition of " bread " shows that it is an actualizing, representational interpretation of the actual bread. The import of Jesus' words is more than that: This bread is his body. Only through the words over the cup is it then clear that Jesus' " body " is seen in a special connection with an event: It is the body of Jesus given up to death (in Luke: " which is given for you "). The question how the " is " is to be understood preoccupied theologians in the age of the Reformation, but in Semitic languages this word (the copula) is not used at all, and consequently the question is framed too narrowly. What has to be grasped is the meaning as a whole in the context of what Jesus did. A weakening of the statement as though Jesus merely intended to compare the bread with his body or to draw attention to his approaching death is excluded by the clear wording (no " as it were "). It is important, however, that he gives the disciples this bread, which he calls his body, to eat; consequently, that is to be understood as implied in the Pauline-Lucan " for you "; it is contained in the " Take " (which is lacking in Paul and Luke). The body of

Jesus, the body delivered up to death, is there for the disciples, is given to them for their salvation, as Paul explains in another passage, " The bread which we break, is it not a participation in the body of Christ? " and " The cup of blessing which we bless, is it not a participation in the blood of Christ? " (1 Cor. 10:16). Bread Eucharist and cup Eucharist explain one another, and only when taken together do they express Jesus' mind completely.

Between the eating of the eucharistic bread and the drinking of the cup, if it was a Passover meal, the eating of the paschal lamb intervened (cf. 1 Cor. 11:25, " after supper "). But there is no mention of this in Mark, and even if the " Lord's Supper " was originally celebrated in the framework of a meal, at an early date the double eucharistic action was moved to the end as a single proceeding (this was probably already so in Corinth). Jesus' further actions are described by Mark almost in the same words as with the bread; only the " breaking " is, of course, omitted, and instead of the prayer stands the Greek word for " thank." In the Passover meal, the third cup is the " cup of blessing "; it comprised all the thanks for the memorial meal. But the name was also given, even at an ordinary festive meal, to the last cup which was drunk with gratitude to God. The Christians adopted this designation for the cup at the eucharistic celebration, as conveying to their minds with particular force the meaning of Jesus' institution (cf. 1 Cor. 10:16a). This cup was handed around, and was therefore a communal cup. At the Passover meal an individual cup for each of the participants was later the rule; but sharing the same cup (especially the " cup of blessing ") is not excluded for Jesus' time. It is a feature of Jesus' special action that he *gives* them the cup and they *all* drink out of this *one* cup. He did not drink from it himself, not in order to renounce wine, but because the cup, which contains his " blood of the covenant," is intended for the disciples. It is to make them share in his blood and in the covenant with God which it establishes.

The words spoken by Jesus over this cup are therefore particularly important. Mark presents a form which is not impossible in Aramaic but is peculiar (literally " the blood of me of the covenant "). This is connected with the fact that the already existing expression " blood of the covenant " is adopted, while at the same time this blood has to be designated as Jesus' blood. The expression comes from Exodus 24:8, where God's Sinaitic covenant is sealed in the blood of the lambs which is sprinkled over the people—a single covenant-forming sacrifice, which nevertheless retains its meaning for all time. For this covenant which God concludes with his chosen people is to endure and its saving power is to be fulfilled in the end (eschatologically) in a perfect community of God with his people. The covenant relationship was repeatedly disturbed in the course of history by Israel's guilt; and for this reason the prophets, Jeremiah especially, promise a new covenant: " Behold, the days are coming, says the Lord, when I will make a new covenant with the house of Israel and the house of Judah, not like the covenant which I made with their fathers when I took them by the hand to bring them out of the land of Egypt . . . But this is the covenant which I will make with the house of Israel after those days, says the Lord: I will put my law within them, and I will write it upon their hearts; and I will be their God, and they shall be my people " (Jer. 31:31–33). Hence the Lucan-Pauline formulation: " This cup is the new covenant in my blood." Both forms of the words over the cup agree in the idea of the covenant. The Sinaitic covenant, which already pointed (typologically) beyond itself, is now fulfilled, and this is the *new* covenant of which Jeremiah had spoken. That is how the Christians understood Jesus' action, even if it is not certain precisely what words he used about the covenant.

The new covenant which Jesus promises to his community is established and sealed by his blood. That is the special idea which could only stand out in full relief when Jesus died; it only became clear and manifest when it was fulfilled. Jesus himself revealed it at this farewell institution, and thus disclosed how he understood the meaning of his death, even if the early Church has elucidated his thought. The reference to the crucifixion is established by the complement of " blood ": " which is poured out." There are no grounds for thinking this refers to pouring out the wine or shedding the blood of the paschal lambs. The verbal form (present participle) is explained as a reference to the event which is imminent: " the blood which is to be poured out." What is imminent is posited for the disciples as present, the saving power of this event is applied to them. The idea of sacrifice is implicit in the memorial of the Sinaitic covenant sacrifice. Above all, the expiatory character of Jesus' death is emphasized, namely by the addition of " for many." This expression introduces the thought of the Servant of God of Isaiah 53 who suffers and dies vicariously " for many."

A further saying is added to the words that institute the covenant, and this announces the ultimate fulfillment of this covenant in the future kingdom of God (v. 25). This eschatological perspective is an essential part of the sacred action instituted by Jesus. His thought of his approaching death receives its purpose and culminating meaning. His death serves to bring about the kingdom of God which he had proclaimed.

It is possible that Jesus did not utter this saying at this point, at the end, but placed the whole festivity, the Last Supper, in this perspective, as Luke 22 : 16–18 suggests. But for the Church's eucharistic celebration it was the meaningful conclusion and culmination, and for Mark's Passion narrative a light ahead. The Church celebrated the Lord's Supper in memory of Jesus' last evening with his disciples as a re-enactment and memorial of his death and in the perspective of his future return. Mark narrates Jesus' action in such a way that the community could feel itself directly addressed. And that also explains why he could dispense with the commission to celebrate the Eucharist: " Do this in remembrance of me." The Church was in fact doing so by celebrating the breaking of bread or Lord's Supper, and did not need Jesus' explicit statement.

The early Church as it celebrated the Eucharist had good reasons for regarding Jesus' actions in the room of the Last Supper as an institution committed to it as a sacred legacy. In particular, Jesus' forward look towards the coming kingdom was a spur at this festive meal to recall to mind again and again the death of the Lord, " until he comes."

THE VISIT TO THE MOUNT OF OLIVES, THE DISCIPLES' DISPERSAL, AND PETER'S DENIAL FORETOLD (14:26–31)

[26]*And when they had sung a hymn, they went out to the Mount of Olives.* [27]*And Jesus said to them, " You will all fall away; for it is written, ' I will strike the shepherd, and the sheep will be scattered.' * [28]*But after I am raised up, I will go before you to Galilee."* [29]*Peter said to him, " Even though they all fall away, I will not."* [30]*And Jesus said to him, " Truly, I say to you, this very night, before the cock crows twice, you will deny me three times."* [31]*But he said vehemently, " If I must die with you, I will not deny you." And they all said the same.*

The walk to the Mount of Olives is attested by all the evangelists. Jesus' visit to the Garden of Gethsemane at the foot of the Mount of Olives and his arrest there, form part of the bedrock of the tradition. Luke and John say that Jesus often went there with his disciples. The garden was situated on the western slope of the Mount of Olives, still within the precincts of Jerusalem where the Passover had to be celebrated. The hymn, too, is readily explained in a Passover setting; it would be the second part of the Hallel (Ps. 115–118), sung after the third cup of wine. It is true, of course, that singing was usual at banquets, but the express mention here is certainly an indication that the narrator was thinking of the Jewish Passover.

During this walk the evangelist places two more grievous announcements by Jesus: the defection of the disciples and Peter's denial. In John's gospel, Jesus tells Peter in the upper room itself (13:36–38), and Luke similarly places it at that point (22:34). It is once again a case of independent items of tradition which were fitted into the continuous Passion narrative, and the mode of presentation betrays the reflection of the early Church. In the center of the announcement that the disciples will all "fall away" ("be made to stumble"), that is to say, will be shaken in faith (cf. 9:42), stands a quotation from scripture, taken from the Hebrew text of Zechariah (13:7), for the Septuagint bears a different meaning ("Strike the shepherds and scatter the sheep!"). The speaker is God, who has the shepherd, his trusted agent, struck so that the "little ones," the obtuse Israelites, may be scattered and so come to their senses and reflect. The saying was admirably suited to interpret the lot of Jesus and his disciples, and already begins to speak in the light of fulfillment. For this reason it is often attributed to the early Church's reflection on scripture.

The next saying (v. 28), which is absent from an ancient papyrus fragment but is probably authentic, must be viewed in close connection with the distressing prophecy. The dispersion of the little flock is followed by their assembly, but only after the death of the shepherd and his raising up by God. The saying itself is explained by 16:7, where the women at the tomb are given a message: "Go, tell his disciples and Peter that he is going before you to Galilee; there you will see him, as he told you." Consequently, the Greek text can hardly be taken to mean, as it could: He will *lead* you into Galilee; for in 16:7 the reunion itself is promised for Galilee. Probably Mark has merged the Easter saying with it, just as the resurrection is always listed with the rest in the prophecies of the Passion (8:31; 9:31; 10:33), and the disciples do not notice this. It is a bright prospect which lights up the darkness of the Passion.

Peter's protest (v. 29) refers to Jesus' saying about all the disciples being scandalized (v. 27a) and amounts to the presumptuous claim that it does not apply to him. Peter trusts to his own strength and thinks himself an exception. For that reason Jesus' prophecy of his triple denial affects him all the more. He, the one who is boasting of his steadfastness, will fail most shamefully. In this picture the hand of the evangelist is visible. The formal structure of the scene is similar to that of 8:31–33: Jesus' announcement, Peter's protest, and the stern reproach and humiliation of Peter by Jesus. This time, however, the evangelist connected up a saying of Jesus which he found in the tradition and which originally had nothing to do with the flight of the disciples (cf. Jn. 13:36ff.; 16:28). The prophecy that this leading disciple will deny Jesus is an early tradition, as its well-worn figurative formulaton shows. The only difference between Mark and the other evangelists is that here Jesus speaks of a double cock crow, in the others only of one. Both are popular expressions for the early hours of the morning (first cock crow about 3 a.m., cf. Mk. 13:35). The second cock crow is probably, in the tradition which Mark adopted, only a figurative way of emphasizing the triple denial (or is the first cock crow a warning to Peter?). "Deny" is a hard saying, according to Luke 12:9, those who deny the Son of man, who do not profess faith in him, will be denied before the angels of God. But Peter goes further in his exaggerated opinion of himself; he says he would rather die with Jesus than deny him. This self-confident assertion is most strongly expressed by Mark, and it was probably he who added that the other disciples said the same. For him, the human presumption and blindness of the disciples are part of the dark mystery of the Passion which Jesus accepts. Jesus says nothing more, and his silence is even more eloquent in prompting the readers to reflect on the delusions to which human pride can lead. Martyrdom itself is a grace, which men can only humbly accept (cf. Jn. 21 : 18f.).

THE AGONY IN THE GARDEN (14:32-42)

[32]*And they went to a place which was called Gethsemane; and he said to his disciples, " Sit here, while I pray."* [33]*And he took with him Peter and James and John, and began to be greatly distressed and troubled.* [34]*And he said to them, " My soul is very sorrowful, even to death; remain here, and watch."* [35]*And going a little further, he fell on the ground and prayed that, if it were possible, the hour might pass from him.* [36]*And he said, " Abba, Father, all things are possible to thee; remove this cup from me; yet not what I will, but what thou wilt."* [37]*And he came and found them sleeping, and he said to Peter, " Simon, are you asleep? Could you not watch one hour?* [38]*Watch and pray that you may not enter into temptation; the spirit indeed is willing, but the flesh is weak."* [39]*And again he went away and prayed, saying the same words.* [40]*And again he came and found them sleeping, for their eyes were very heavy; and they did not know what to answer him.* [41]*And he came the third time, and said to them, "Are you still sleeping and taking your rest? It is enough; the hour has come; the Son of man is betrayed into the hands of sinners.* [42]*Rise, let us be going; see, my betrayer is at hand."*

E

This grave narrative now opens the story of the Passion. Jesus intends to spend the time until the traitor approaches in personal prayer. The Son of man is entering into the complete solitude in which he prays to the Father. His purpose recalls the temptation in the desert (1 : 13), and even more his prayer in the lonely place at the beginning of his ministry (1 : 35). On that occasion he prayed early in the morning for clarity about his course, now, in the darkness of the night, to be able to endure the end. However, he takes his three disciples a little farther towards the place where he will pray. Even on the way, still in the disciples' presence, horror and mortal anguish overwhelm him; it is only then that he says, " Remain here and watch " (v. 34). They may and must realize Jesus' extremity of weakness and distress; one day they will have to make known both his mysterious suffering and his resurrection. Jesus' agony is expressed in the words of a psalm. The phrase " my soul is sorrowful " occurs frequently; in Psalm 42:6, 12, it expresses the inner distress in which the suppliant longs for the presence of God, in Psalm 43:5, he laments in the face of powerful enemies and pleads with God to vindicate his cause. Jesus goes further, however, and says, " even to death," not as though in deepest sadness he would rather be dead (cf. Job 3), but because he has come to the threshold of death (cf. Lk. 22:44). Similarly in a Qumran psalm we find: " My soul within me languishes even unto death " (1 QH 8:32).

It is not said that Jesus sought consolation from the presence of the disciples; they are to watch. This watching, in this kerygmatic account, does not mean that they are to be on the look-out to report anything suspicious, or even keep enemies at bay. It is connected with the reproach to Peter (v. 37) and with the exhortation to watch and pray (v. 38). It means interior vigilance in the hour of crisis. Nor is it said that the disciples are to watch *with Jesus*, although it fits the situation (only

Matthew adds it). Mark avoids such an addition because for him the Son of man watches, prays, suffers, and is in agony alone. Accordingly, Jesus goes a little farther, away even from those closest to him, falls on the ground and prays.

The prayer in direct speech is completely in accord with the mind of Jesus. Abba, " Father," or " my Father," was the way Jesus addressed God. The evangelist adds the Greek translation, as Paul does in Galatians 4:6 and Romans 8:15. ("Our) Father " is also the way the Church addresses God, as Jesus taught it. Consequently, Jesus' prayer on the Mount of Olives cannot but remind the community of its own prayer, and tells it that God the Father is still powerful to help in the greatest human distress. " All things are possible " with him, as has already been said in Mark 10:27 in an exhortation to the disciples, a saying which echoes from the Old Testament into the New (Gen. 18:14; Job 42:2; Zech. 8:6; Lk. 1:37). Jesus prays to the Father to take this cup from him. What is meant is not the mental anguish of that moment but the coming Passion. The cup, originally a metaphor for the cup of wrath or stumbling which God gives his enemies to drink, can also denote the death which God inflicts on his faithful. Jesus shrinks in horror from the mortal suffering, but adds, " Not what I will, but what thou wilt." He remains the obedient Servant of God. God's will may not be annulled.

The sleeping disciples form a painful contrast to Jesus praying in his agony. Jesus addresses his reproach to Peter, who had been so boastful earlier (v. 31); he had been willing to go to death with Jesus, and now cannot even watch one hour. Once again Mark avoids a " with me "; he should have watched, not for Jesus' sake, but because he himself is in peril. But the same applies to all the disciples and the faithful of later times. And so the exhortation to the disciples (v. 38) extends the situation then to the condition of the Christian in the world generally and becomes an exhortation to all: "Watch and pray that you may not enter into temptation." It is the same thought as in the Lord's prayer, the same word for the situation of peril to salvation which can become superhumanly strong—"temptation" not to this or that sin, but to apostasy from God and consequent loss of salvation.

The next two verses merely serve to show that Jesus' prayer continued in three stages. He prays in the same way as before (v. 39) and then finds the disciples asleep; their weariness is some excuse (v. 40). On the third occasion, only his return to the disciples is mentioned, and a remark that can be construed either as a reproachful question (" So you are still sleeping and resting? ") or as an ironic exclamation. The next word in the Greek, linguistically disputed, marks the end; the RSV translation " It is enough " (Vulgate: *sufficit*) is only one possibility among others. For the evangelist, however, the words about the Son of man are important, for taken with verse 21 they under-line his Christological view: the Son of man accepts the destiny laid down for him, now that the hour has struck. With the command to get up and follow him—not to flee, but to meet the traitor—the evangelist shows that Jesus is facing what is to come with composure. Jesus has endured his agony, mastered it in prayer to the Father, and goes forward calmly and with dignity to meet those who will seize him and lead him away.

JESUS' ARREST AND THE DISCIPLES' FLIGHT (14:43-52)

43And immediately, while he was still speaking, Judas came, one of the twelve, and with him a crowd with swords and clubs, from the chief priests and the scribes and the elders. 44Now the betrayer had given them a sign, saying, " The one I shall kiss is the man; seize him and lead him away safely." 45And when he came, he went up to him at once, and said, " Master! " And he kissed him. [46]And they laid hands on him and seized him. [47]But one of those who stood by drew his sword, and struck the slave of the high priest and cut off his ear. [48]And Jesus said to them, " Have you come out as against a robber, with swords and clubs to capture me? [49]Day after day I was with you in the temple teaching, and you did not seize me. But let the scriptures be fulfilled." [50]And they all forsook him, and fled. [51]And a young man followed him, with nothing but a linen cloth about his body; and they seized him, [52]but he left the linen cloth and ran away naked.

Scarcely has Jesus spoken of the " hour " and the approach of the traitor, than the latter " immediately " arrives. It is pointless to ask about the circumstances, for example whether the other disciples had noticed nothing, or whether the three Jesus was speaking to had got up. All that is important is that " while he was still speaking " the traitor arrived with the band of police. Now the unfaithful disciple is named and once again designated as " one of the twelve " (cf. 14:20). Jesus' prophecy at supper has been fulfilled, and also his other prophecy that the Son of man must be rejected by the elders and the chief priests and the scribes (8:31). For in his description of the crowd that comes to effect the arrest, Mark makes a point of emphasizing that it was sent by the various groups represented in the Sanhedrin. He expressly names them, but in a different order, because the chief priests and scribes are the driving forces. Swords and clubs are the normal weapons; the slaves of the Sanhedrin were notorious for their wooden cudgels, as we know from a satirical song in the Talmud. Mark also specifies the weapons because of Jesus' words in verse 48.

Some exegetes consider that as a prearranged signal Judas' kiss is improbable, because there was no need for it; a word to the temple police would have been sufficient. The fourth evangelist does not mention it. But that greeting from the traitor is not necessarily unhistorical on that account; Judas and the enemies of Jesus wanted to make quite sure in the dark of night (cf. v. 44). The misuse of the friendly greeting is emphasized by Mark by the strong expression he uses, but he records no reply on Jesus' part. The hypocritical gesture leads to Jesus' immediate arrest. Only now is there a reaction from a bystander. There is no need to speculate whether it was perhaps someone who was not one of the disciples. In the course of the narrative Jesus' companions realize what is going on only when Jesus has already been arrested. There is no fight, but one of those present draws his sword and strikes the slave of the high priest. It is a mere episode that has no effect on the course of events. Only in Matthew and John does Jesus say something to the man who had struck the blow; Mark has refrained from commentary.

Instead, he reports Jesus' words to those who have arrested him, " Have you come out as against a robber with swords and clubs to capture me?" It is plain that this is also Christianity's answer to the Jewish leaders who were responsible. The secret arrest of Jesus by the Jewish authorities is an indisputable fact. At most it can be questioned whether, as the fourth evangelist reports, in addition to the Jewish temple police, a Roman detachment with its captain was not involved as well (cf. Jn. 18:2, 12). Historically it is more likely that the operation was carried out by the Jewish authorities, perhaps after informing the Roman occupation forces. Mark's intention in giving Jesus' answer is to point out the infamous and cunning procedure used by the Sanhedrin. Jesus had taught openly in the temple and they had not arrested him. The readers of the gospel are prepared for this; it has already been said several times that the leaders were trying to destroy Jesus but feared the people (11:18; 12:12;

14:1f.). They have come out as against a " robber "; it is not really possible to infer from this expression that Jesus was arrested as a resistance leader or insurrectionist, even though Barabbas, who according to Mark 15:7 certainly was one, is also called a " robber " at John 18:40. What kind exactly the two men were who were crucified with Jesus, and who are also called "robbers" (Mk. 15:27), we do not know. Brigandage was widespread in Palestine in those days, so the word is probably best understood in that connection. Mark sees Jesus' answer as manifesting the same humiliation and indignity as in his crucifixion between two " robbers." Yet outrage and shame, rejection by the leaders of the people, are the lot assigned to the Son of man (cf. 8:31).

The disciples' flight ensues; all of them abandon Jesus. To insult by enemies is added abandonment by friends. A young man, who had probably been sleeping nearby, followed the band with the arrested man or, rather, correctly speaking followed " him," that is, Jesus. This probably indicates that the young man became a disciple of Jesus, and was later a member of the community. But the evangelist is simply describing graphically the scene at that moment. Clad only in a linen cloth, the young man is seized, but leaves the linen cloth and escapes. Perhaps the first readers may have known who the evangelist meant, as with the Simon of Cyrene who had to carry the cross beam for Jesus and who, the evangelist says, was the father of Alexander and Rufus (15:21). In that case it may rightly be assumed that they were members of the Church later. There is, however, no firm foundation for the frequent suggestion that the young man was John Mark, the evangelist himself. After the flight of the disciples, this little incident is intended to show that even this " follower " of Jesus finally fled. The Son of man goes his way absolutely alone.

The Proceedings against Jesus (14 : 53—15 : 15)

Voluminous works have been written about the trial of Jesus, and there is no sign of the argument coming to an end. Anyone dealing with the historical question of this trial, which in fact people would like to reopen even today, finds himself faced by almost insuperable difficulties. This is bound up with the fact that our only sources are the gospels. No documents in the case have been preserved, though there is a fictitious and worthless account in an apocryphal work (the *Acts of Pilate*). The accounts in the gospels are not only incomplete, they exhibit considerable divergences. How could the Christians, it may be asked, gain precise information about the secret Jewish proceedings and the trial before Pilate? Finally, for the historian and jurist, the gospels are suspect of bias of various kinds due to the subsequent beliefs of the Christian community and evangelists, intensified by contemporary prejudices against Judaism and the Roman State. According to how one estimates the historical value and reliability of the gospels, judgment varies between complete acceptance of the events reported in them (the divergences between the gospels having then to be reconciled), and complete rejection, in particular of the Jewish proceedings against Jesus. Even the trial before Pilate is received critically. Between the two alternatives lie all kinds of positions which it is impossible even to enumerate here.

Is it possible to read Mark's account of the trial with spiritual profit, without going into this learned controversy? The believing reader cannot push these questions aside entirely, for even in the trial the purpose and ministry of the earthly Jesus find expression. Nor can it be a matter of indifference to a believing Christian whether the Jews were right, on whatever grounds at all, to deliver up Jesus to the Roman court, and whether the

Roman judge was right to condemn Jesus as a resistance leader and insurrectionist. At least one point must be decided: whether it was a miscarriage of justice, one of the most terrible and influential judicial errors in history, for if those who regard the verdict of the Roman judge as justified are right, Christianity in its entirety would be nothing but a delusion, an ideology that arose after the event but has practically nothing to do with the Jesus of history. Early Christianity wanted to bring to light the human injustice that had been done to Jesus, by tracing the course of his trial; yet ultimately it wanted to do more. For it was filled with the deep conviction of faith that God himself had vindicated Jesus, by raising him from the dead, and that he will give him his full rights eventually at the parousia when he brings him as the Lord and the judge of the world (cf. Mk. 14:62). This hidden judgment, passed by God on the unbelieving world, is disclosed by John from his theological viewpoint (cf. Jn. 16:8-11). But Mark and his community already know of this deeper meaning; our evangelist represents it in his own way when he emphasizes the saving plan according to which the Son of man must be "rejected" by men, and when he presents Jesus as the just man who, though innocent, suffers and enters into deepest darkness and even in the greatest dereliction is still God's beloved Son, and from the most shameful death comes to the resurrection. Anyone who sees things in this way will understand that the early Church was not concerned with a verbatim report of the trial. It certainly did not intend to give a merely imaginary account either, but wanted to elucidate matters historically to a sufficient extent to prove Jesus' innocence even on the human, historical plane. But provided this was credibly demonstrated, the strictly historical interest was exhausted, and the presentation tends towards the theological background to which we have referred. This is what we shall have to be particularly attentive to, without losing sight of the question whether the conviction of the early Church regarding Jesus' human innocence and the guilt of his judges was historically well founded.

THE PROCEEDINGS BY NIGHT BEFORE THE SANHEDRIN (14:53–65)

⁵³And they led Jesus to the high priest; and all the chief priests and the elders and the scribes were assembled. ⁵⁴And Peter had followed him at a distance, right into the courtyard of the high priest; and he was sitting with the guards, and warming himself at the fire. ⁵⁵Now the chief priests and the whole council sought testimony against Jesus to put him to death; but they found none. ⁵⁶For many bore false witness against him, and their witness did not agree. ⁵⁷And some stood up and bore false witness against him, saying, ⁵⁸" We heard him say, ' I will destroy this temple that is made with hands, and in three days I will build another, not made with hands.' " ⁵⁹Yet not even so did their testimony agree. ⁶⁰And the high priest stood up in the midst, and asked Jesus, " Have you no answer to make? What is it that these men testify against you? " ⁶¹But he was silent and made no answer. Again the high priest asked him, "Are you the Christ, the Son of the Blessed? " ⁶²And Jesus said, " I am; and you will see the Son of man sitting at the right hand of Power, and coming with the clouds of heaven." ⁶³And the high priest tore his mantle, and said, " Why do we still need witnesses? ⁶⁴You have heard his blasphemy. What is your decision? " And they all condemned him as deserving death. ⁶⁵And some began to spit on him, and to cover his face, and to strike him, saying to him, " Prophesy! " And the guards received him with blows.

The evangelist's hand is immediately evident in the formal structure of this account of the nocturnal session of the Sanhedrin, the highest Jewish judicial authority, which has given rise to so much discussion. Just as in the pericope about the raising of the daughter of Jairus and the woman with the hemorrhage (5:22-43), he interweaves two narratives, the judicial proceedings with Peter's denial (cf. vv. 54 and 66-72). At least, the reader is prepared by verse 54 for what happens later in the courtyard. The two happenings are deliberately juxtaposed and contrasted. While Jesus faces his earthly judges and is ill treated, he is denied by the disciple who had protested he would go with him even to death. The structure of the Jewish proceedings is very similar to the trial before Pilate: many accusations, Jesus' silence, question from the judge, Jesus' answer, verdict, mockery. Nevertheless, the specific character of the two procedures is maintained and the different coloring of each conveyed. Nor can it be denied that a markedly Christian viewpoint is evident. The aim is to demonstrate Jesus' innocence by the fruitless interrogation of witnesses, to confront Jesus' answer—that is the culminating point—with the challenge to the high priest's questions, and the entire proceedings are concluded by an undignified scene of mockery.

The question remains, of course, what capital crime the highest Jewish court held Jesus to have committed, and it is scarcely possible now to determine this with full historical certainty. If we understand " blasphemy " in a wider sense, as we are justified in doing for that period (the Mishnah lays down limiting conditions), the issue was a religious conflict between Jesus and leading circles in Judaism. It was a mortal conflict, and according to Mark and the other early Christian writers (cf. Jn. 19:17), one that inevitably sprang from Jesus' mission.

After his arrest, Jesus is brought " to the high priest " where the members of the Sanhedrin are assembled. The palace (house) of the high priest which appears at first sight to be meant was situated, according to tradition, in the upper city (on Mount Zion). However, since there is no other evidence that the Sanhedrin held its sessions there, it is more probable that its usual meeting place is meant, but it is no longer possible to determine where this was. The evangelist emphasizes that " all " the chief priests, elders, and scribes were present, the official representatives of Judaism. The " courtyard " of the high priest (the word can also mean the palace), into which Peter makes his way, is represented as an inner yard where the servants have lit a fire against the chill of the night. This description serves merely as preparation for the story of the denial. Since we hear that Peter had "followed him at a distance," we must not regard the disciples' flight as implying they left Jerusalem and returned at once to Galilee. All these features, however, the vague references to place and the absence of reference to time (perhaps between two and three o'clock in the morning), the way the members of the Sanhedrin are summoned at this hour, indicate that the evangelist is not concerned with graphic description but with theological aspects.

The examination of witnesses was a characteristic of Jewish legal procedure, as can be studied in the story of Susanna. There had to be at least two witnesses whose testimony agreed even in details; the man or woman accused need not be questioned at all (Sus. 50); but cross-examination of the witnesses may follow (Sus. 55–63). Later on, inquiries were demanded (seven questions into the circumstances) and as many cross-examinations (into details) as desired were permitted. Mark, however, describes the hearing of the testimony in a summary way, and emphasizes the following aspects, which are what he is interested in: The Sanhedrin " sought " to find some capital crime of which Jesus was guilty, but without success; there were " many " witnesses, but they bore false witness and their allegations did not agree. Only one concrete piece of evidence was adduced, the saying about the temple which has already been mentioned more than once (cf. 13:2). Here Mark is certainly working over a tradition. Jesus must have made some statement at some time on this subject, but it is no longer possible to reconstruct its tenor, for the versions are very diverse (weaker in Mt. 26:61: "I *am able* to destroy the temple of God . . .; different again Jn. 2:19; Acts 6:14). Mark again emphasizes that it was false testimony. He also immediately gives an interpretation by additions (not found in the other gospels): the temple " made with hands " and another temple " not made with hands." It is clear that he is thinking of the building of God's Church; the community as new temple, as eschatological temple of God.

The examination of witnesses proved fruitless and puts the high priest in a predicament. So to induce Jesus to make some ill-considered statement, he steps forward and asks him, Are you making no answer to what they testify against you? Jesus' silence defeats this attempt. It has been thought that this silence, which is repeated before the Roman judge (15:4f.), is intended to recall Isaiah 53:7, which says of the Servant of God, " He opened not his mouth, like a lamb that is led to the slaughter . . ." Now, at last, the president of the court, who with all its members is seeking grounds for condemnation, has hit the right note. Jesus faces up to the question, and his answer, which acknowledges his messiahship—not, it is true, in a Jewish but in a Christian sense—makes possible the sentence of death.

The accompanying scene of mockery illustrates the crime of blasphemy of which Jesus is guilty in the eyes of these Jews. In the circumstances, it is the members of the council themselves who spit on him contemptuously and deride him as a false prophet by covering his face, striking him, and demanding that he say who did it. A distinction is drawn between them and the guards, who brutally strike his face. Historically, of course, this scene before the highest Jewish tribunal is scarcely conceivable. But the evangelist and the primitive Christian tradition before him narrated this to demonstrate the unbridgeable antithesis, stirred up by passions, between Jewish unbelief and Christian faith in the Son of God.

PETER'S DENIAL (14:66–72)

⁶⁶*And as Peter was below in the courtyard, one of the maids of the high priest came;* ⁶⁷*and seeing Peter warming himself, she looked at him, and said, " You also were with the Nazarene, Jesus."* ⁶⁸*But he denied it, saying, " I neither know nor understand what you mean." And he went out into the gateway.* ⁶⁹*And the maid saw him, and began again to say to the bystanders, " This man is one of them."* ⁷⁰*But again he denied it. And after a little while again the bystanders said to Peter, " Certainly you are one of them; for you are a Galilean."* ⁷¹*But he began to invoke a curse on himself and to swear, " I do not know this man of whom you speak."* ⁷²*And immediately the cock crowed a second time. And Peter remembered how Jesus had said to him, " Before the cock crows twice, you will deny me three times." And he broke down and wept.*

Mark's account deliberately rises to a climax. In face of the maid who recognizes Peter and accuses him of belonging to the followers of the " Nazarene " Jesus (probably a name for his place of origin), Peter pretends to know nothing and to be at a loss. He claims not to understand what she is talking about at all. The second time when she discovers him in the forecourt, and tells others what she suspects, he denies again. But when the bystanders become insistent, because they recognize him as a Galilean (by his speech), he begins to curse and to swear that he does not know " this man." The curses invoked on himself, the oaths, and the contemptuous way of referring to Jesus, all show how far Peter has sunk and entangled himself in sin.

Then the cock crow brings him to his senses and, shattered by his failure, he begins to weep.

The story is self-sufficient, yet fits into the whole. Mark certainly composed it deliberately in that way. First of all he wants to show how Jesus' prediction was fulfilled. That is evident from the way he points out that Peter "remembered." Secondly, the evangelist depicts Peter's failure in clear contrast to Jesus' courageous attitude. While Jesus confesses he is the Messiah, the Son of man, incurs the death sentence, and is mocked as a blasphemer, Peter is denying his association with Jesus before a maidservant and guards. Finally, the evangelist is emphasizing once again the warning to the community which it had already been urged to take to heart when Jesus made the prediction: to build on one's own power and strength is illusory and dangerous. Even a slight occasion can bring human presumption to a fall; one must follow Jesus with courage on his way and ask for strength not to succumb to temptation.

THE TRIAL BEFORE PILATE: CHARGE AND INTERROGATION (15:1-5)

[1]*And as soon as it was morning the chief priests, with the elders and scribes, and the whole council held a consultation; and they bound Jesus and led him away and delivered him to Pilate.* [2]*And Pilate asked him, "Are you the King of the Jews?" And he answered him, "You have said so."* [3]*And the chief priests accused him of many things.* [4]*And Pilate again asked him, "Have you no answer to make? See how many charges they bring against you."* [5]*But Jesus made no further answer, so that Pilate wondered.*

By the expression " and as soon as," the evangelist links the previous section with the trial before Pilate. The indication of time, "it was morning," appears to link up well with the second cock crow (14:72) but in reality it opens a new narrative, which Mark wants to connect with the Jewish trial. It is early morning (about six o'clock) as the Sanhedrin " came to a decision," " prepared their decision." The Greek expression might also be translated " held a consultation " (RSV) or " held a council," and this has led to discussions whether a second session of the Sanhedrin was held. That is improbable in view of the short time that had elapsed; moreover, it would mean that the subject discussed would not be referred to at all by Mark, and it would also clash with the Lucan account which speaks of only one session, though in the morning (22:66). Mark must have thought that the meeting in the night had lasted into the early hours of the morning and the Sanhedrin now arrived at the decision to deliver up Jesus to the Roman tribunal. This does not necessarily mean that this corresponds to the historical course of events (cf. above, introduction to the trial of Jesus). What concerns the evangelist is that the highest Jewish authorities, the " whole council " as he adds by way of additional emphasis after listing the groups represented in it, arraigned Jesus before a Roman tribunal. The politically responsible chief priests are singled out, but all the representatives of the nation are behind the decision and therefore collaborate in the condemnation of Jesus by the Gentiles. Jesus is fettered, not only for security but also as a sign that he is regarded as a dangerous criminal, a rebel. The expression " they delivered him " here primarily means " they brought him before the court, arraigned him " (cf. 13:9, 11), but for Mark it also has the deeper theological implication that the Son of man is delivered into the hands of sinners (9:31; 10:33; 14:41).

Roman law courts began their proceedings at dawn. In contrast with Jewish procedure, which chiefly consisted in hearing testimony, those indicted before a Roman court were themselves interrogated. In the provinces, except for Roman citizens, the procedure was simpler than in the strict criminal law of the Roman State. We hear only later (v. 3) of the charges brought by the chief priests, and then only in summary form. This shows once again that the evangelist's aim is not to unfold the precise course of the proceedings but simply to focus attention on what is most important for him. The charge presupposed is clear from Pilate's question: "Are you the King of the Jews?" Jesus has therefore been accused of claiming to be the messianic king, which in the eyes of the Roman means a nationalist insurgent and political rebel. Luke, who places the charge at the beginning, explains: He perverts our nation, forbids payment of tribute to the emperor, and says he is the messianic king. Pilate can at most have asked, "Do you call yourself the King of the Jews?" But Mark intentionally uses the wording he does in order to present the decisive question in the sharpest light.

The parallel to the high priest's question—the culminating point in the proceedings before the Sanhedrin—is unmistakable; but the differences, too, are equally evident; in the former, the question about the Messiah, the Son of the Blessed in the religious sense; here, the question of the King of the Jews on the political plane. Similarly in regard to Jesus' answer: there, a clear affirmation of Messiahship ("I am"), even if expanded for Christian understanding; here, a reserved answer ("You have said so"), which implies an affirmation but even more clearly includes a proviso. For Jesus cannot say he is the "King of the Jews" in the sense the questioner understands this designation, yet it is correct, on another plane. The early Christian recognition of Jesus' kingship cannot be excluded from Mark. The condemnation, and even more the mocking, of Jesus as the "King of the Jews" (15:10–20; cf. 15:32) to his mind probably contained the same sort of hidden truth as the words of the evil spirits. But Jesus does not explain his kingship to the Roman (a different account is given in John's gospel). The brief answer suffices. Pilate would not have been able to understand more.

The many charges brought by the chief priests vividly suggest their efforts to get Jesus condemned to death, but are not listed. From the narrator's point of view their function is to make Jesus' silence stand out more insistently and strikingly. Jesus makes no further answer; and this fact is emphasized by Pilate's astonishment. Undoubtedly Jesus' silence corresponds to his actual conduct before the Roman judge (cf. also Jn. 19:9f.), but it probably has a theological significance. What did Jesus' silence signify to the early Church and to our evangelist? At this point an allusion to the Song of the suffering Servant of God (Is. 53:7) might be intended, but this is by no means certain. It might imply contempt for the Jews, who are bringing unfounded, calumnious accusations, as the false witnesses did before their own court. But Mark, with his Son-of-man theology, will have seen an even deeper meaning in it: Jesus makes no attempt to refute the charges alleged against him, so as to follow the path laid down for him. Perhaps Pilate's astonishment indicates that a mysterious dignity and authority radiate from Jesus. But the account is too concise to affirm with certainty that an interpretation of this kind is present, as it is in John's gospel. Jesus' silence forms part of the picture of the Son of man, misunderstood and condemned, calumniated and hated by men yet aware of his fate and accepting the mysterious sufferings in obedience to the will of the Father.

THE RELEASE OF BARABBAS AND THE CONDEMNATION OF JESUS (15:6-15)

⁶*Now at the feast he used to release for them one prisoner whom they asked.* ⁷*And among the rebels in prison, who had committed murder in the insurrection, there was a man called Barabbas.*

[8]*And the crowd came up and began to ask Pilate to do as he was wont to do for them.* [9]*And he answered them, " Do you want me to release for you the King of the Jews? "* [10]*For he perceived that it was out of envy that the chief priests had delivered him up.* [11]*But the chief priests stirred up the crowd to have him release for them Barabbas instead.* [12]*And Pilate again said to them, " Then what shall I do with the man whom you call the King of the Jews? "* [13]*And they cried out again, " Crucify him."* [14]*And Pilate said to them, " Why, what evil has he done? " But they shouted all the more, " Crucify him."* [15]*So Pilate, wishing to satisfy the crowd, released for them Barabbas; and having scourged Jesus, he delivered him to be crucified.*

The Marcan account displays a tendency to attribute responsibility for Jesus' condemnation to the chief priests. They stir up the crowd to demand the release of Barabbas and the crucifixion of Jesus. Pilate's compliance with the shouts of the mob is, of course, no excuse or vindication of the Roman procurator and judge. But the account does not aim at completely exculpating the Roman. Here too theological considerations are present. Jesus is passed over in favor of a rebel implicated in murder and is condemned to a criminal's death. The Son of man falls " into the hands of sinners " and falls victim to a combination of human weakness and malignity. Pilate too is for Mark one of the human beings who is guilty of Jesus' death but who at the same time accomplishes God's hidden design.

There is no proof of a regular amnesty granted to a convict on a high festival, but some traces of a practice of this kind have been found. The Roman historian Livy speaks of a mass amnesty on a feastday (V, 13, 8) and a papyrus reports a trial in Egypt in A.D. 85 in which a governor released a criminal at the wish of the people. Now a crowd goes up to the fortress Antonia (or to Herod's palace if the Roman governor resided there) and demands their " right." Pilate attempts to persuade them to choose Jesus the " King of the Jews," in order to help him solve what is otherwise an awkward case for him. It is also said that he realized that the chief priests had brought Jesus before his court " out of envy." The expression does not occur elsewhere in Mark; it probably means that they were envious of the great following that Jesus attracted, or at all events were swayed by selfish, impure motives. But the chief priests stir up " the crowd," inhabitants of Jerusalem, their supporters, to ask for the release of Barabbas.

A few indications are given about this Barabbas, who at Matthew 27:18 in some manuscripts is also called " Jesus "—Barabbas would then be the surname " son of Abbas." He belonged to a group who had started an insurrection obviously quite a short time before and had committed a murder in the course of it. Smaller outbreaks of this kind were frequent, and were mostly soon suppressed by the Romans with much bloodshed. We have no precise information about this resistance group and their uprising. Any link with Luke 13:1 or speculation about an uprising at the Feast of Tabernacles is extremely questionable. Nothing points to Jesus' having any connection with these rebels. If the early Church wanted to gloss over revolutionary activity on Jesus' part, it would have been ill-advised to relate the Barabbas incident at all.

In Mark, the move for a Passover amnesty comes from the crowd, and this is probably more likely than the offer that Pilate himself makes according to Matthew 27:17 and John 18:39. The Roman judge is only using this as an opportunity of getting rid of Jesus. But the mob is egged on by the chief priests and demands the release of Barabbas. Pilate's further question as to what he is to do with Jesus leads to the cry, " Crucify him." This is the only place in the gospel in which the " crowd " shows hostility to Jesus; but it must be remembered that what is meant here is a particular crowd of people in the service of the chief priests, not the great throng which gladly heard him in the temple (12:38), and certainly not the Galilean crowd in Jesus home country. In Mark, all the responsibility falls on the chief priests, nevertheless this cry of "crucify him," which becomes a fanatical shout when the governor once again intervenes on Jesus' behalf, remains a terrible sign of how far hatred can lead. For Mark, this is a further fulfillment of Jesus' saying that the Son of man must be "rejected." Pilate yields to the pressure of the crowd, releases Barabbas, and "delivers" Jesus to be put to death by crucifixion. Of the actual formal verdict we hear nothing, but a single word informs us that Jesus was also scourged.

The brevity with which the end of the trial is related is very striking, and confirms that the early Church was not concerned with reporting the precise course of the trial but primarily wanted to present Jesus' Passion. And despite its knowledge of the cruelty of the punishments of that age, this earliest account does not linger over the physical tortures, which of course many other men had to endure in those days, but lays the stress on the injustice done to its innocent Lord. The rebel Barabbas goes free, Jesus must take the way of the cross. The scourging is mentioned in connection with the crucifixion; in fact it was a usual preliminary in order to weaken the condemned man and make the torments of crucifixion even more unbearable. The Roman scourging, which could also be inflicted as an independent punishment (cf. Lk. 23:22), or was used to obtain an admission of guilt (so perhaps at Jn. 19:1), was a flogging with the "scourge" (*flagum*), a whip of leather thongs or iron chains, loaded with bone or metal. It probably took place in the interior of the praetorium. It was the beginning of Jesus' physical sufferings, in which he was spared none of the tortures which human beings have devised for their fellow men. Roman writers themselves only mention crucifixion with terror and abhorrence, as a death reserved for criminals, slaves, and rebels.

Way of the Cross, Death, and Resurrection (15 : 16—16 : 8)

The break we are making after the condemnation of Jesus in order to follow him now on his way to the foot of the cross is an artificial one for the sake of clarity. In the Marcan account, the mockery by the Roman soldiers follows at once; after this brief interlude we move directly from the tribunal to the place of execution. This is due once again to the fact that Mark was not interested in giving a formal report of the trial—the verdict is not even mentioned—but wants to describe Jesus' Passion. For the same reason we do not expect any information about the details of the execution, but, rather, a picture of Jesus' sufferings presented to the Church and designed to bring out its deeper meaning as the suffering of this innocent man unjustly condemned, this just man persecuted, the Son of God dying utterly forsaken. As well as all the physical sufferings, he has to endure mockery and sneers and even experience abandonment by God. But with his death, which is marked by a loud cry, a change sets in. The curtain of the temple is torn in two, the Gentile centurion confesses that " this man was the son of God," and the women present already point for the reader to Easter morning. Jesus also receives honorable burial, and then after the sabbath quiet comes the women's visit to the tomb, and the message of the resurrection rings out.

In this last part of the Passion narrative, then, the theological treatment is unmistakable. The community receives a vivid exposition, setting the past event before its eyes, of its confession of faith that Jesus " died and was buried and on the third day was raised " (cf. 1 Cor. 15 : 3f.), though without the interpretation which faith alone certifies, that he " died for our sins," for that could not be directly represented in the narrative. The other addition in that old creed, " in accordance with the scriptures," is expressed as far as it was possible to do so in the account of Jesus' suffering and death, not through formal fulfillment texts, but by hidden scriptural reference, in Jesus' last words, even by quoting the psalm verse in the Aramaic language. There are references to psalms which express the sufferings of the just man, which the early Church understood messianically, that is, applied to its dying Messiah. These psalms of the distress of just men who are persecuted and humiliated emphasize above all the interior suffering, to which the early Church was deeply sensitive.

MOCKERY OF JESUS AS THE KING OF THE JEWS (15:16–20a)

[16]*And the soldiers led him away inside the palace (that is, the praetorium); and they called together the whole battalion. [17]And they clothed him in a purple cloak, and plaiting a crown of thorns they put it on him. [18]And they began to salute him, " Hail, King of the Jews!" [19]And they struck his head with a reed, and spat upon him, and they knelt down in homage to him. [20a]And when they had mocked him, they stripped him of the purple cloak, and put his own clothes on him.*

After sentence has been passed, the Roman guard amuse themselves by their cruel mockery of Jesus as the " King of the Jews." The " whole battalion " (cohort) is not the permanent garrison of the fortress Antonia, but the guard which the governor usually brought from his palace by the lake in Caesarea for the great festivals, which easily led to unrest and excitement among the crowds of pilgrims in the capital. What is pointed out now as the *lithostroton*, a large stone pavement (Jn. 19:13), would, if the localization is correct, be the site of the tribunal close to the fortress Antonia. The Roman soldiers perhaps included Syrian auxiliaries, who were well known for their hatred of the Jews. That would even more readily explain the crude and spiteful mockery of the " King of the Jews "; the Jews themselves avoided that title, preferring to speak of the " King of Israel " (15:32).

The incident itself is vividly related. The soldiers put a purple cloak on Jesus, perhaps an old red-colored soldier's cloak, and plait a wreath of thorns on his head. There were many thistle and thorny plants in Palestine. There is no need to imagine big sharp thorns; some commentators suggest the thorny *poterium spinosum* with its small blood-red flowers. The soldiers were more intent on ridicule than on inflicting bodily pain. Purple cloak, diadem, and scepter were royal insignia which they were derisively mimicking, so they must certainly have put the reed in his hand first (Mt. 27:29) before taking it from him and striking him with it. They insulted him with homage such as the great and distinguished pay to a king. But the scene degenerates brutally; they spit on him ignominiously and strike him with the reed. All this is told without extenuation but also without exaggeration, and not a word is said about Jesus' behavior. He is the helpless victim of brutal soldiery.

WAY OF THE CROSS AND CRUCIFIXION (15:20b–27)

²⁰ᵇ*And they led him out to crucify him.* ²¹*And they compelled a passerby, Simon of Cyrene, who was coming in from the country, the father of Alexander and Rufus, to carry his cross.* ²²*And they brought him to the place called Golgotha (which means the place of a skull).* ²³*And they offered him wine mingled with*

myrrh; but he did not take it. ²⁴*And they crucified him, and divided his garments among them, casting lots for them, to decide what each should take.* ²⁵*And it was the third hour, when they crucified him.* ²⁶*And the inscription of the charge against him read, " The King of the Jews."* ²⁷*And with him they crucified two robbers, one on his right and one on his left.*

A description of crucifixion was not necessary to people of that time. At the place of execution there were usually posts which served as uprights; the condemned men themselves had to carry the crossbeams. They were nailed or bound to this with outstretched arms and then raised on the upright. The walk to the place of execution with the heavy beam on their shoulders meant great toil and pain for the condemned, weakened as they were by the scourging. The place was outside the city walls; Jesus, too, " suffered outside the gate " (Heb. 13 : 12). Its name is uniformly transmitted as " Golgotha " and translated as " skull." Probably it owed this name to its shape. At that time, however, Golgotha, the " skull," was simply the equivalent of the Gallows Hill of our medieval towns.

Jesus must have been so weakened that the soldiers compelled a man who happened to be coming from the country to carry the crossbeam for him. There was no legal basis for such forced labor—little the soldiers cared. The early Christian tradition preserved this man's name: Simon. He had probably lived earlier in Cyrene (in North Africa) where there was a big Jewish colony, and then in later years, like many pious Jews, had settled in Jerusalem (cf. Acts 2 : 10; 6 : 9). Only Mark names his two sons, Alexander and Rufus, who were known as Christians in the (Roman?) Church (cf. the Rufus in Rome, Rom. 16 : 13). For the carrying of the cross he uses the same verb (" take up ") as in the saying about discipleship (8 : 34). Luke expresses it even more plainly: they " laid on him the cross, to carry it behind

Jesus " (23:26). Simon thus becomes a model for the Christian reader. John, however, omits this feature, and says in accordance with his own Christology that Jesus bore his own cross (19:17). This was probably the case at the beginning of the walk; but Mark's statement shows a feeling for historical detail.

The wine spiced with myrrh was an opiate to enable the victim to endure the terrible tortures. It is attested as a Jewish custom, but not otherwise known among the Romans. It is possible that Jewish women had this bitter drink prepared and that the soldiers allowed them to offer it to Jesus. But Jesus did not take the wine, and this in the evangelist's view certainly indicates that Jesus willed consciously to endure the sufferings and death. Matthew notes that he tasted it but would not drink (27:34). The later offer of a drink of watered vinegar had a different purpose, but at an early date was interpreted in terms of Psalm 69 (68):22. Both incidents were understood in the light of that psalm as ill-usage. Once again Mark is nearer the historical truth with the myrrhed wine; but he also links a theological consideration with Jesus' refusal.

The crucifixion itself is not described; tact and good taste forbade the early Church from doing so. Jesus' utter poverty, however, is indicated by an incident which is historically indubitable: the soldiers' casting lots for Jesus' clothes. The victim's clothes were a perquisite of the execution squad. This sharing out and casting lots for Jesus' garments reminded the early Church of a passage in the psalm (Hebrew 22, Greek 21) which in general seemed to express Jesus' Passion. It is the agonized prayer of a tormented man who is heard and saved from deepest distress and who, in the last part of the psalm, brings a thanks offering to God. Already in Mark the words are assimilated to the Greek text (Ps. 21:19), although the fulfillment of scripture as such is not pointed out. That is how the early Church and, with it, Mark, represented Jesus' Passion. For informed readers the facts appeared in a new light through the words of scripture, the background of the divine design opened out and made the terrible event to some slight degree intelligible.

The time of the crucifixion (third hour = 9 a.m.) was probably inserted subsequently, whether by the evangelist or an early copyist. Coming after the casting of lots for the garments, it is awkward, and names once again the crucifixion (cf. v. 24a); it also conflicts with John 19:14, which states that sentence was passed at the sixth hour. Half-way between the two might represent the actual hour. In Mark, a three-hour pattern is recognizable (cf. v. 33); is this intended to hint at God's plan which stands behind it all? If verse 25 were omitted, Jesus could have been crucified about noon, and the darkness would have set in soon afterwards. More important in the basic account is the tablet setting out the grounds of condemnation, which was displayed on the cross, probably over the head of the crucified. The name Jesus is not mentioned in Mark and Luke, but will not have been omitted. The old Passion narrative was chiefly concerned with the title " King of the Jews " which represented Jesus as a political insurgent and yet in a deeper sense expressed the truth. The fourth evangelist understood this, developed it in his account of the trial, and emphasized it by the special attention he gives to the superscription (three languages, protest by the Jews: Jn. 19:19–22).

The two men crucified at the same time are mentioned in all the gospel accounts; there can be no doubt that Jesus hung on the cross and died between two other condemned men. It is more difficult to say what kind of persons they were. In Mark and Matthew they are called " robbers," in Luke 22:33, " criminals." The Greek word Mark uses serves in Flavius Josephus to denote nationalist rebels; yet that is not sufficient reason to regard these men as insurgents who had perhaps taken part in the insurrection mentioned at 15:7. The release of Barabbas scarcely supports this; at all events the source narrative knows nothing of this and seems to regard them as ordinary robbers. The very fact that Jesus was crucified between two criminals was recognized to be a fulfillment of scripture, namely of what is said in the Servant Song: " He was numbered with the transgressors " (Is. 53 : 12). But only Luke mentions this text, and not in the Passion narrative but in the room of the Last Supper (22 : 37). In Mark, this fulfillment text follows at the end of this section only in some manuscripts (as v. 28); but the verse certainly does not belong to the original text of Mark but was inserted by thoughtful copyists on the basis of the Lucan passage. The original account simply lets the facts speak, and what they say is harsh enough: the Son of God was executed like a common criminal.

JESUS' SUFFERINGS ON THE CROSS AND HIS DEATH (15 : 29–37)

[29]And those who passed by derided him, wagging their heads, and saying, " Aha! You who would destroy the temple and build it in three days, [30]save yourself, and come down from the cross! " [31]So also the chief priests mocked him to one another with the scribes, saying, " He saved others; he cannot save himself. [32]Let the Christ, the King of Israel, come down now from the cross, that we may see and believe." Those who were crucified with him also reviled him. [33]And when the sixth hour had come, there was darkness over the whole land until the ninth hour. [34]And at the ninth hour Jesus cried with a loud voice, " Elo-i, Elo-i, lama sabach-thani? " which means, " My God, my God, why hast thou forsaken me? " [35]And some of the bystanders hearing it said, " Behold, he is calling Elijah." [36]And one ran and, filling a sponge full of vinegar, put it on a reed and gave it to him to drink, saying, " Wait, let us see whether

Elijah will come to take him down." [37]*And Jesus uttered a loud cry, and breathed his last.*

The tradition about the " passersby "—Simon himself was coming in from the country—has preserved the memory that Golgotha was not far from a city gate, through which many people were passing in and out. This, too, argues that it was the day before the Passover. But the remark is just as unemphatic as the " all who saw me " in Psalm 21:8; their mockery here is called " derision," perhaps intentionally, because this word is frequently used elsewhere for blasphemy (cf. 2:7; 3:29; 14:64), and in the text of the psalm a different word is used. For Mark, it is blasphemy of the Son of man who will one day come with divine power.

The darkness which falls " over the whole land " from the sixth to the ninth hour, was not a natural eclipse of the sun. Even in antiquity that was known to be impossible at the time of the full moon (Passover). Consequently, other commentators have suggested a darkening of the sun by sandstorms (" black sirocco "); but a natural explanation is hardly to be looked for. As the expression " over the whole earth " shows (even if it is translated " over the whole land "), a symbolic event is meant, the mourning of creation at the drama which is unfolding on Golgotha.

The culmination of Jesus' Passion is represented by the loud and agonizing cry with which he laments his abandonment by God. Here, the early Church even transmitted a Semitic text, not in the original Hebrew text of Psalm 22:2, but in Aramaic. This tradition therefore certainly goes back to the Aramaic-speaking Jewish-Christian community; Mark has preserved Aramaic sayings in other passages (5:41; 7:34; 10:51). Matthew has changed the wording, in particular he gives the address to God in Hebrew (Eli), probably because otherwise the confusion with

Elijah is incomprehensible. It is disputed whether Jesus himself uttered the cry in Aramaic or Hebrew. But the fact that the early community transmitted Jesus' words in the Aramaic language with which it was familiar, suggests that it not only wanted to show Jesus using that psalm as his prayer, but also took the content of this introductory verse of the psalm very seriously. Consequently, the grave import of these words should not be weakened by saying that Jesus was reciting a psalm which moves on from deepest dereliction to thanksgiving and praise for deliverance, or that he was struggling through from desolation to complete trust, or even that his emphasis in his prayer was on the end of this psalm. No one can know what Jesus' state of soul really was; but the early Church's intention in quoting this psalm verse was to express deep distress of soul and abandonment by God. For Mark, it is the dregs of the cup which, in Gethsemane, Jesus had prayed to the Father might pass from him. Jesus' dereliction in this hour of darkness is unfathomably deep. " With a loud voice " he cries in uttermost distress " to him who was able to save him," as we also read in Hebrews 5 : 7.

Some of the bystanders who heard it thought he was calling on Elijah. The crucified did not hang very high above the ground and were guarded by soldiers. It is not said that the misunderstanding was a malicious one. If these people had understood correctly the cry to God, and had wanted to be spiteful, they would have had even more reason for derision. We must assume that a genuine reminiscence has been preserved here. The confusion with Elijah does of course presuppose that Jesus uttered at least the address to God, even perhaps the whole verse, in Hebrew, which the people did not understand. Elijah was regarded in Judaism as a helper in many needs. No messianic significance of the great prophet, who was awaited as the forerunner of the Messiah and the restorer of all things (cf. 9 : 12), is to be seen here. Jesus, those people thought, was calling upon Elijah as a helper in need. Thereupon one man runs, dips a sponge in " vinegar " and says, " Wait, let us see whether Elijah will come to take him down." The man's motive is not entirely clear. It may have been an impulse of sympathy for the thirsty man, but it could also be intended to prolong his life. In Matthew it is the others, not the man who put the sponge to Jesus' lips, who say " Wait, let us see whether Elijah will come to take him down," and this is another taunt. Luke represents the action as done by soldiers in mockery (23:36).

Crucified men often lingered a long time on the cross; the saddle block supported their bodies, until they finally died of suffocation. This makes Jesus sudden expiry and the loud cry which he uttered shortly before his death all the more surprising. There has been much discussion of the physical cause of Jesus' death. Some doctors think exhaustion, others a traumatic shock and heart failure. But there can be no doubt about the rapid and sudden death accompanied by the loud cry. How did Mark understand this cry? Is it the same as the one previously articulated in the words of the psalm (v. 34)? Did he accordingly understand it as an expression of profound distress and desolation, even of despair? Matthew regards it simply as another cry (27:50). If Mark viewed it in the same way, he may have interpreted this final wordless cry as a sign of conquest and victory. In support of this is the immediate reaction of the Roman centurion, who confesses " Truly this man was the Son of God! " Thus Jesus would have been delivered from deepest dereliction by God and his vindication by God would have been intimated even in his death. In the light of the psalm whose opening verse Jesus recites, this interpretation is a likely one, since the end of the psalm speaks of deliverance by God. But as far as Mark is concerned, no psychological interpretation should be suggested, as though by reciting that psalm Jesus had attained triumphant trust in God. Mark does not intend to lessen the extreme darkness, the inner distress of the Son of man, but to express the actual dying itself as deliverance and vindication by God, the snatching of the Son of God from the power of death.

Jesus' last utterance on the cross, which later by the addition of the sayings handed down by the various evangelists became Jesus' " seven last words " on the cross, can no longer be established with any certainty. Each evangelist compiled sayings of the crucified in his own way and each gives a particular meaning to Jesus' last utterance or cry. The only firm ground is probably that loud cry, of which the oldest tradition speaks, a cry which was unusual in a crucified man and strongly affected the bystanders. We should accept the mystery and bow before the majesty of this death, whether we regard it as the last revelation of Jesus' humanity or as a hidden sign of his closeness to God and of his divinity. The mystery of a human life deepens or is disclosed on the threshold of death; in the death of this One, the whole mystery of his person and earthly ministry confronts us once more. Then both ways of regarding it are valid; whether the depth of his humanity or the hidden reality of his divinity shines out, will also depend on our own sensitivity.

EVENTS FOLLOWING JESUS' DEATH (15:38–41)

[38]*And the curtain of the temple was torn in two, from top to bottom.* [39]*And when the centurion, who stood facing him, saw that he thus breathed his last, he said, " Truly this man was the Son of God!"* [40]*There were also women looking on from afar, among whom were Mary Magdalene, and Mary the mother of James the younger and of Joses, and Salome,* [41]*who, when he was in Galilee, followed him, and ministered to him; and also many other women who came up with him to Jerusalem.*

The importance and significance of the hour when Jesus breathed his last is emphasized by certain items handed down by the early Church. Again we must ask what meaning they had for Mark. The first is the rending of the veil of the temple, an event which is obviously understood to bear a symbolic meaning. What is referred to may be the inner veil which separated the Holy of Holies from the Holy Place, or the outer veil on the front of the temple; the Greek expression could mean either. Because of the strong symbolism, many commentators think that Mark means the inner veil; but even apart from the fact that if it were rent, this could not be publicly known, there are other reasons for thinking that the outer veil is meant, which was visible to visitors to the temple. According to Jewish tradition, the western lamp went out forty years before the destruction of the temple, and the doors of the temple, closed in the evening, were found open in the morning. This was regarded as a calamitous portent. This tradition need not be directly connected with the event recorded by Mark, but it perhaps throws light on the early Church's standpoint: the veil which hid the sanctuary from view and protected the sanctity of the temple, is torn, the previous order of worship is at an end, the old covenant ceases. In Jewish speculation this (outer) veil of the temple had an additional meaning, as representing the created universe. Now this cosmic significance, the meaning of Christ's death for the whole universe, seems to be implied at least for Matthew, for he links other events with it—an earthquake takes place, the rocks are rent, tombs open, the bodies of dead saints are raised—all signs of the end of the world, of eschatological deliverance. Mark probably regarded the rending of the veil of the temple simply as a sign from God, or as a calamitous portent pointing to the end of the ancient cult.

In contrast to this, the confession of the Gentile centurion assumes high positive significance for the Gentile world, especi-

F

ally for the Gentile Christian readers of Mark's gospel. This unprejudiced witness of Jesus' death professes, " Truly this man was the Son of God." The special manner of his death—probably the loud cry is meant—has impressed this Gentile who stood facing the cross, and he sums up his impression in words which in his mind probably meant little more than: He was an extraordinary, a " divine " man (Luke: He was a just, that is, an innocent, man). But the Christian community hears in this utterance the confession of faith in Jesus' divine sonship as the Church itself understands it. For Mark, it is the highest attribute and dignity, appropriate to Jesus alone (cf. 1:11; 9:7; 12:6). It had never previously been attributed to Jesus by any human being (the high priest had merely inquired about it). Consequently, this confession of the Gentile centurion is a culminating point, heralding at this moment of Jesus' death the great turning point which has now arrived; it foreshadows the full profession of faith of the Church when it has come to know Jesus' resurrection. In Jesus' death the mystery of his person, his divine sonship, is revealed.

The women who watch from afar and whose names are listed have a different role—they appear as representatives of the community of believers. These women have already " followed " Jesus in Galilee and ministered to him; others, too, are mentioned, who had gone up to Jerusalem with him. Jesus' disciples could not be added, they had fled, but there were some faithful people who at least watched " from afar." Mark is drawing on existing tradition here, for the three women named appear again in the account of the visit to the tomb (16:1), and in the same order: Mary Magdalene (=of Magdala), another Mary, described as the mother of James the " small " (either because of his stature or because of his age) and of Joses and Salome.

This is the only mention in Mark's gospel that women had followed Jesus in Galilee and " served " him, ministered to his daily needs, but this is confirmed by another, independent passage in Luke 8:2-3. Here, the third evangelist lists other women, and names one of them Joanna (the wife of Chuza) with the other women who visited the tomb (24:10). According to John 19:26, Jesus' mother and her sister also stood by the cross. Women did not count as witnesses in the Jewish view, nevertheless they were important to the early Church because of the historical role they played in the discovery of the empty tomb. Two of these women are also named at the burial, but probably that is a special account. For Mark, who combined these traditions, the women accompany Jesus along his whole way, in Galilee, on his journey up to Jerusalem, then from cross to tomb, until on Easter morning they are given the message: He is risen, he is not here (16:6). They are silent, but for faith eloquent, witnesses of these uniquely memorable events.

THE BURIAL OF JESUS (15:42-47)

[42]*And when the evening had come, since it was the day of Preparation, that is, the day before the sabbath,* [43]*Joseph of Arimathea, a respected member of the council, who was also himself looking for the kingdom of God, took courage and went to Pilate, and asked for the body of Jesus.* [44]*And Pilate wondered if he were already dead.* [45]*And when he learned from the centurion that he was dead, he granted the body to Joseph.* [46]*And he bought a linen shroud, and taking him down, wrapped him in the linen shroud, and laid him in a tomb which had been hewn out of the rock; and he rolled a stone against the door of the tomb.* [47]*Mary Magdalene and Mary the mother of Joses saw where he was laid.*

Only an influential man could have succeeded in obtaining the body of a crucified man. Joseph of Arimathea is described as a respected member of the council who " took courage " to go to Pilate. His native place Arimathea can no longer be located with certainty, but probably lay in Judea; perhaps it was Rentis, seven miles or so northeast of Lydda. He is described as " looking for the kingdom of God "; he had obviously been impressed by Jesus' preaching; according to John 19:38, he was " a disciple of Jesus, but secretly, for fear of the Jews." Now, however, he shows courage, for Pilate was known for his harshness. The governor's surprise at hearing that Jesus was already dead is convincing, for crucified men often lingered for a long time. However, the centurion confirms that death has already taken place. When the corpse is granted, Joseph buys a linen shroud. The expression used does not necessarily mean that he wrapped Jesus' body in a single large cloth, and need not conflict with the Johannine statement that they bound the body of Jesus in " linen cloths [or bands] " (19:40; cf. 20:6). But there is no mention of anointing; for Mark the saying at the anointing in Bethany (14:8) remains valid.

The body of Jesus is laid in a tomb hewn out of the rock. Such rock graves were common; they were entered through a low opening into a burial chamber with niches in the side walls to receive the bodies. The other evangelists add that it was a new grave (Mt.) in which no one had yet lain (Lk.) and that it was in a garden close by (Jn.). Joseph of Arimathea secured the entrance to the rock tomb with a big stone, probably a rolling stone, which worried the women on their way to visit the tomb (16:3f.). Additional details are not important to the source account; only one further point is noted, that Mary Magdalene and Mary the mother of Joses saw where the body was laid. The fact that the second Mary is designated differently from 16:1 and that only two women are mentioned is probably a sign that the account of Jesus' burial was originally narrated separately.

For the evangelist, however, the last observation is a link with the story which follows concerning the discovery of the empty tomb.

THE EMPTY TOMB AND THE ANNOUNCEMENT OF THE RESURRECTION (16:1–8)

¹And when the sabbath was past, Mary Magdalene, and Mary the mother of James, and Salome, bought spices, so that they might go and anoint him. ²And very early on the first day of the week they went to the tomb when the sun had risen. ³And they were saying to one another, " Who will roll away the stone for us from the door of the tomb? " ⁴And looking up, they saw that the stone was rolled back; for it was very large. ⁵And entering the tomb, they saw a young man sitting on the right side, dressed in a white robe; and they were amazed. ⁶And he said to them, " Do not be amazed; you seek Jesus of Nazareth, who was crucified. He has risen, he is not here; see the place where they laid him. ⁷But go, tell his disciples and Peter that he is going before you to Galilee; there you will see him, as he told you." ⁸And they went out and fled from the tomb; for trembling and astonishment had come upon them; and they said nothing to anyone, for they were afraid.

Only after the strict sabbath rest could the women buy spices. The sabbath ended at sundown, but it was then too late anyway to hurry to the tomb. Consequently, the women set off very early the next day. The note " on the first day of the week " is noteworthy, for everyone else the resurrection is " on the third day " or " after three days." Those are a proclamation formula whereas the words here state an actual time. The narrative, therefore, can hardly have been constructed out of that credal formula; consequently the primitive tradition knows that on the first day of the week the women went to the tomb, even if it is not clear why they did so. Did they merely want to perform an additional act of piety? Did they simply go to see the tomb, as Matthew says, probably for reasons similar to those we have been considering? Matthew, of course, with his story of the guard posted at the tomb and the sealing of the tomb (27:62–66) himself created a new difficulty. In fact, no anointing does take place in Mark, so that the women's intention does not annul Jesus' prophetic statement at 14:8. But Mark can hardly have invented the three women himself; they are the same three who are named as present at the crucifixion.

Their anxiety on the way about who will roll aside the stone sounds plausible, yet one wonders why they did not think of this before setting out. Besides, it most probably was a cylindrical stone which one man could move, and most certainly three women. But rational considerations of this kind miss the point of the story. If the scene is closely scrutinized, the explanatory clause " for it was very large " is also very clumsy, for they have already looked up and seen the stone is rolled back (a few manuscripts reverse the order). These verses are, rather, a stylistic means of heightening the tension. The women arrive at the tomb, go in, and find that Jesus' body is no longer there.

The story of the young man in a white robe, in the circumstances clearly an angel, a messenger of God, must have been told very early. If the account was to disclose to the community the meaning it bore for faith, Jesus' resurrection itself had to find expression. This is the angel's function. He announces the message of Jesus' resurrection at the empty tomb. He is an *angelus interpres,* or spokesman interpreting the event to which the empty tomb bears witness. Such a conception is not only legitimate as consonant with the mode of expression of biblical literature, but is clearly correct when the divergences in the other evangelists are taken into consideration. In Luke, two men address the women, who bow their faces to the ground, in words which differ considerably from those in Mark. The commission to the disciples to go to Galilee is omitted, in accordance with the theological tendency of this evangelist to leave the disciples in Jerusalem. In John, Mary Magdalene does indeed see the two angels sitting at the head and foot of the place where the body of Jesus had lain, but they do not announce the resurrection to her; Jesus himself appears and does this. The meeting of the angel and the women is narrated in Mark in the style proper to such announcement scenes. The women are frightened at the sight of this messenger from another world, and he calms them: Do not be amazed. Then the announcement follows. The first sentence can be either a statement or a question: "You seek Jesus of Nazareth [the man of Nazareth (cf. 10:47; 14:67)], the crucified? He has risen, he is not here." The empty tomb as such is not a direct and unambiguous testimony to Jesus' resurrection; in the words of the angel, however, it becomes a speaking witness: "See the place where they laid him." If the scene with the angel is regarded as a figurative, concrete representation of what the empty tomb means, the latter does not lose its evidential value, though it does move to second place in regard to faith in the resurrection. That is fully in accordance with the view of the early Church. In the early credal formula of 1 Corinthians 15:3ff., the empty tomb is not mentioned (but it is stated that Jesus was buried, and that means that he entered completely into the realm of the dead); it is the appearances of the risen Christ which are the basis of belief. Only in connection with the appearance of Jesus crucified and risen has even the empty tomb its meaning and evidential value. In the view of the people of that time, Jesus' body could not remain in the tomb if he had risen. But it was not through reflections on this that the story of the empty tomb was arrived at; the historical fact will be that on Easter morning the women of Jerusalem discovered the empty tomb and, with the disciples, attained faith in Jesus' resurrection when the appearances followed. In retrospect, the empty tomb also became evidence for the resurrection for the early Church as well, and this testimony is expressed by the angel's announcement. It was not dead stone but the living Jesus who awakened the Easter faith; but the tomb is an earthly document of the non-earthly event.

The message which the angel gives the women for " his disciples and Peter " is part of the Easter announcement, because it points to the appearances of the risen Christ. Without these, as we have seen, there would not have been any firm Easter faith, and no real conception of the meaning of the risen Christ and his resurrection reality. If we understand the kerygmatic character of the narrative, it becomes of secondary importance whether perhaps an original account contained no reference to the angel's commission to the women.

Attempts have been made to explain historically the behavior of the women in fleeing in fear and astonishment, on the supposition that it was prompted simply by their discovery of the empty tomb; their " trembling and astonishment "—in the Greek two strong expressions are used—would have been a natural reaction to the terrible discovery they had just made. In John's gospel, Mary Magdalene, who at first simply thinks that Jesus' body has been removed, begins to weep (20:11, 13, 15), which after all seems a more likely reaction. Furthermore, if this explanation were correct, we should rather expect the women to run straight to the disciples (cf. Jn. 20:2). The reaction in question is more easily explained if the women had undergone an experience of quite a different kind, such as the angelic apparition with the inconceivable announcement of Jesus' resurrection. Mark describes a similar reaction at the raising of the daughter of Jairus: " And immediately they were overcome with amazement " (5:42). It is the " ecstasy," provoked by the numinous, a *mysterium tremendum*: to be beside oneself because of a supernatural happening. That is how Mark will have understood it. That would also explain why the women " said nothing to anyone "; the fear which the brief final sentence gives as an explanation is their awe and agitation in face of the numinous (cf. 4:41 after the stilling of the storm on the lake: " And they were filled with awe "). The other evangelists have made it less abrupt: " with fear and great joy they ran to tell his disciples " (Mt. 28:8); " returning from the tomb they told all this to the eleven and to all the rest " (Lk. 24:9). It is scarcely possible now to penetrate to the historical facts of the case.

The Greek sentence ends with an explanatory participle, " as a matter of fact," " you see." This is a harsh construction but not impossible. To this day it is disputed whether the whole gospel could have ended in this way, or whether what followed has been lost or replaced. Reasons can be suggested in support of both. There was no absolute need for a continuation, because Jesus' resurrection has been announced and the appearances have at least been fore-shadowed. The women's awe mirrors the incomprehensible, powerful, overwhelming message: Jesus the crucified has risen.

The Longer Ending of Mark (16:9–20)

⁹Now when he rose early on the first day of the week, he appeared first to Mary Magdalene, from whom he had cast out seven demons. ¹⁰She went and told those who had been with him, as they mourned and wept. ¹¹But when they heard that he was alive and had been seen by her, they would not believe it. ¹²After this he appeared in another form to two of them, as they were walking into the country. ¹³And they went back and told the rest, but they did not believe them. [14]*Afterward he appeared to the eleven themselves as they sat at table; and he upbraided them for their unbelief and hardness of heart, because they had not believed those who saw him after he had risen.* [15]*And he said to them, "Go into all the world and preach the gospel to the whole creation.* [16]*He who believes and is baptized will be saved; but he who does not believe will be condemned.* [17]*And these signs will accompany those who believe: in my name they will cast out demons; they will speak in new tongues;* [18]*they will pick up serpents, and if they drink any deadly thing, it will not hurt them; they will lay their hands on the sick, and they will recover."* [19]*So then the Lord Jesus, after he had spoken to them, was taken up into heaven, and sat down at the right hand of God.* [20]*And they went forth and preached everywhere, while the Lord worked with them and confirmed the message by the signs that attended it. Amen.*

The appearance of the risen Christ to Mary Magdalene " early on the first day of the week," which does not link up very well with the account of the discovery of the empty tomb, is compiled from John 20:11–18 without additional details. Mary Magdalene is also described from Luke 8:2 as the woman from whom Jesus had driven out seven demons. That should not be interpreted as implying great sinfulness (the sinner of Luke 7:36–50 can hardly be the same person); the serious possession signifies, rather, a calamitous illness from which Jesus had healed her. The author only means to introduce Mary Magdalene to the readers, he is not concerned with deeper characterization. Consequently, he does not mention her weeping when she found the body of Jesus was no longer there. He does, however, describe Jesus' companions mourning and weeping as though lamenting the dead. They do not believe the woman's message. The word for " appeared " is different from the one used in other texts, and expresses a realistic, bodily manifestation, and the whole passage displays a heavy, more material mode of thought.

With similar brevity the Emmaus story from Luke 24 is recapitulated. That precious and profound narrative is reduced to Jesus' appearing " in another form " to " two of them," that is, of the companions of Jesus just mentioned (who are probably thought of as quite a large group) as they were walking in the country. In the view of the author, Jesus had deliberately assumed the form of a stranger; he says nothing about the two disciples at Emmaus having their eyes opened in the breaking of bread. Once again the only important point for him is that the other disciples did not believe.

Finally, the author speaks of the appearance of Jesus to the " eleven "; he clearly has in mind the description in Luke 24 : 36–43, where it is also a question of the disciples' unbelief. As the unknown author of this appendix conceives it, Jesus himself blames their unbelief and hardness of heart once again, because they did not credit those who had seen him, the risen Christ. The scarcely veiled intention is to show the readers the necessity of willing belief. But the disciples are shown in an unfavorable light. This prompted yet another copyist to insert an explanation and excuse. This little dialogue between the disciples and Jesus, preserved in a single Greek manuscript of the fourth or fifth century, is worthy of note because of its attitude of mind, its grim view of the world and the power of Satan. It runs as follows: And they replied saying, This age of lawlessness and unbelief is under Satan, who by means of evil spirits prevents the true power of God from being apprehended; therefore reveal thy righteousness now. They were speaking to Christ, and Christ said to them in reply: The limit of the years of the authority of Satan has expired, but other terrible things are coming, even for sinners on whose behalf I was delivered over to death, that they might turn to the truth and sin no more, in order that they may inherit the spiritual and incorruptible glory of righteousness, which is in heaven.

The sending of the disciples to preach the gospel also belongs for Matthew (28:16–20) and Luke (24:47) to the Easter appearance of the risen Christ. The author of the longer ending emphasizes the world-wide ministry of the mission, comprising the whole creation. It is not meant that the disciples are to preach to the irrational creation, for the next sentence speaks of the faith by which every human being must respond. But the victorious advance of the gospel is envisaged, just as in the hymn to Christ of 1 Timothy 3:16: " preached among the nations, believed on in the world." This Church is assured that only those who believe and are baptized will be saved, that anyone who does not believe will be condemned at God's judgment. Special emphasis also falls on the promised miracles; this, too, probably echoes the experience of the missionary Church, in which charismatic wonderworking forces were operative. It has been noted that all the cures and miracles listed also occur in the Acts of the Apostles. But the harshness of the condemnation of the unbelievers, where no distinction is drawn between willful and excusable, and the insistence on the marvels which accompany the mission are historically conditioned features to which we must not attribute an absolute significance for all time.

Finally, Jesus' ascension and enthronement at the right hand of God are spoken of. The Lucan picture of Jesus' bodily departure has prevailed, although it was merely a form of representation, unknown to the other evangelists. But it presented no difficulty in the world picture of that age, and made it possible to imagine Jesus leaving the disciples yet at the same time remaining close to the Church. The Lord sitting at the right hand of God remains linked with the Church on earth which continues his work, and he helps it by his collaboration, which the author again sees particularly exemplified in the signs which support the missionary preaching. The missionary impulse that derived from the risen Christ is also clear in another, much shorter, ending to Mark's gospel which is found in a number of manuscripts: " But they reported briefly to Peter and those with him all that they [the women] had been told. And after this, Jesus sent out by means of them, from east to west, the sacred and imperishable proclamation of eternal salvation."

The gospel which Jesus had announced during his earthly ministry was to become a vital and saving force for mankind only after he was delivered up to death. His Church, however, which after the death of its Lord is conscious of the duty to preach the gospel incumbent on it, knows that it is not sent to do so by its own strength, but by the authority of the risen Christ. He himself continues his preaching through the Church, which has the certainty of victory within it because of his resurrection from the dead.